I0467282

London Ontario in Colour Photos, Saving Our History One Photo at a Time

Photography
by Barbara Raué
2012

Series Name:
Cruising Ontario

Book 48: London in Colour

Cover Picture: Talbot Street Baptist Church erected in 1881.
It is now a Christian Reformed Church.

Series Name: Cruising Ontario
Saving Our History One Photo at a Time

Photos now in full colour
Check the Appendixes in the back of each book for
descriptions of architectural terms and building styles

Book 33: Southampton
Book 34: Jarvis
Book 35: Hagersville
Book 37: Simcoe
Book 38: Cambridge Part 1 – Galt Book 1
Book 39: Cambridge Part 1 – Galt Book 2
Book 40: Cambridge Part 2 – Preston
Book 41: Cambridge Part 3 – Hespeler
Book 42: Kitchener Book 1
Book 43: Kitchener Book 2
Book 46: Shelburne
Book 47: Alton
Book 48: London in Colour
Book 50: Orangeville Beginnings
Book 51: Orangeville on Broadway

Other Books by Barbara Raue

Coins of Gold

Arrows, Indians and Love

The Life and Times of Barbara
Volume 1: Inventions That Have Enhanced My Life
Volume 2: Entertainment That I Have Enjoyed
Volume 3: East Coast Trips
Volume 4: Olympics Have Always Intrigued Me
Volume 5: Wonders of the World
Volume 6: Caribbean Cruises We Have Enjoyed
Volume 7: Animals
Volume 8: Storms and Other Major Disasters in My Lifetime
Volume 9: Wars, Terrorist Attacks and Major Disasters

The Cromwell Family Book

Visit Barbara's website to view all of her books
http://barbararaue.ericraue.com

London, Ontario

In 1793 on the River Thames, Lieutenant-Governor John
Graves Simcoe selected a site for the capital of Upper Canada.
York (Toronto) became the seat of government, but in 1826
London was selected as the judicial and administrative center
of the London District. A courthouse and gaol (1829) and
homes for the government officials were built, stores and
hotels were opened. A British garrison stationed at London in
1838 stimulated its growth. The Thames River in southern
Ontario begins near Tavistock and Mitchell and flows 273
kilometers southwest to Lake St. Clair. The river winds
through Carolinian forests, farmlands, rural and urban
communities.

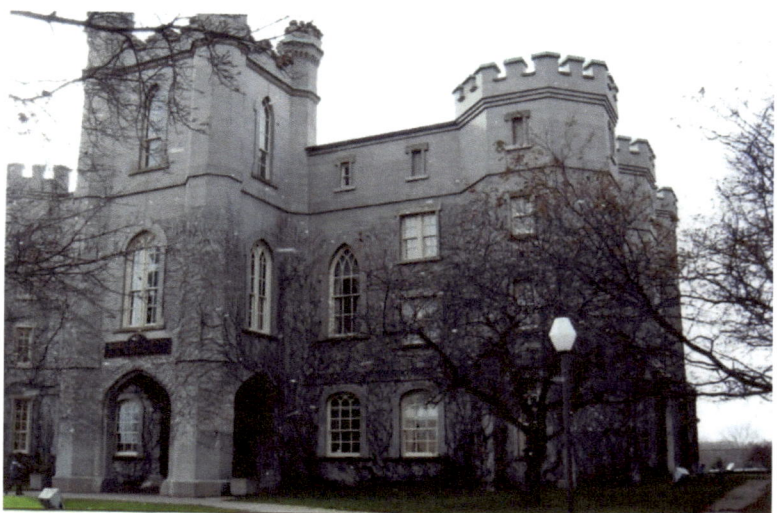

Middlesex County Court House erected in 1830, modeled after
Malahide Castle near Dublin, Ireland, the ancestral home of
Colonel Thomas Talbot, founder of the Talbot Settlement.

Department of National Defense Wolseley Barracks
Now – Royal Canadian Regiment Museum
Oxford and Elizabeth Streets

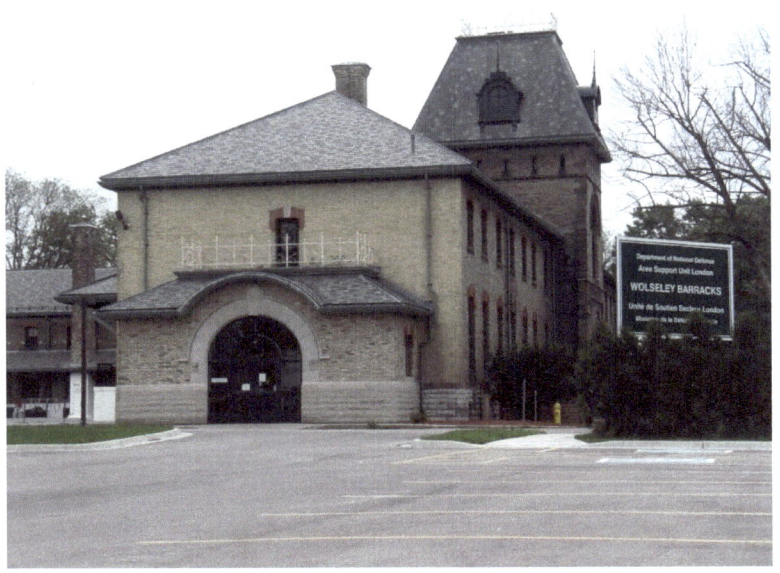

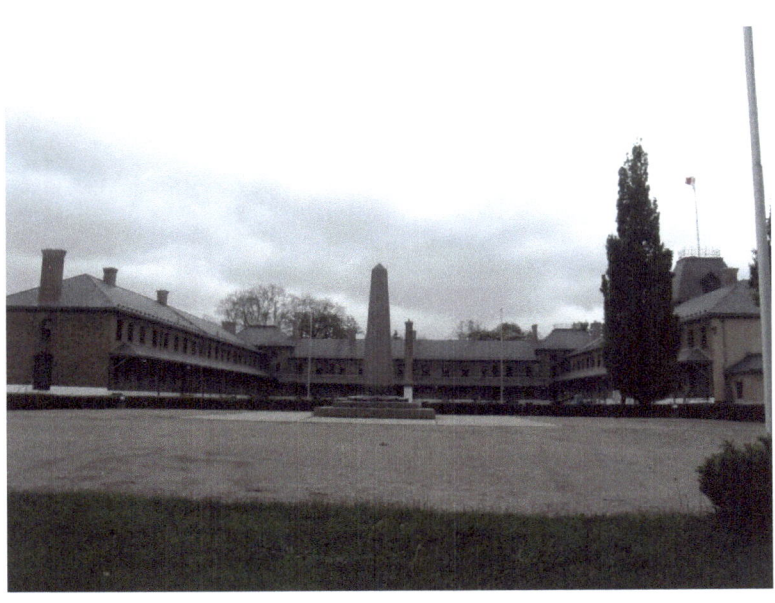

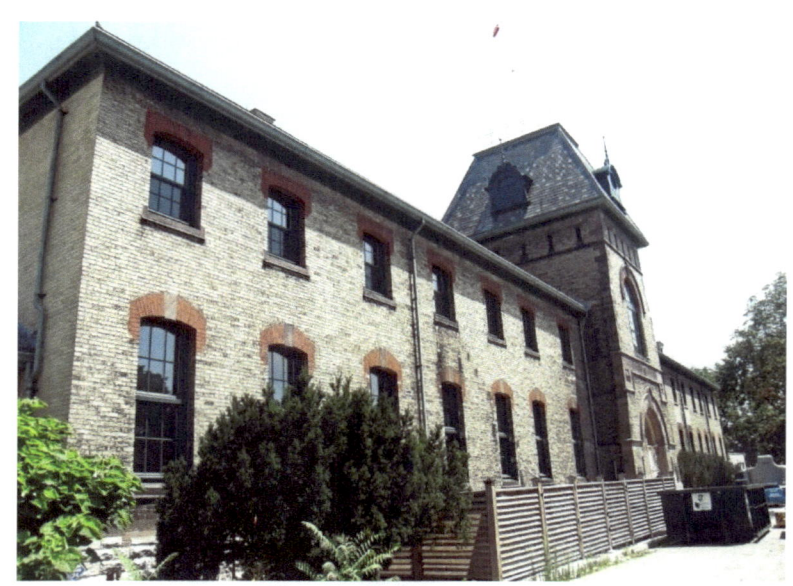

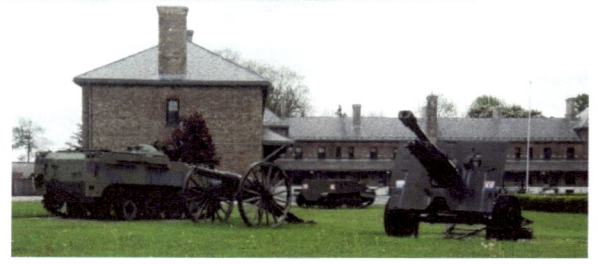

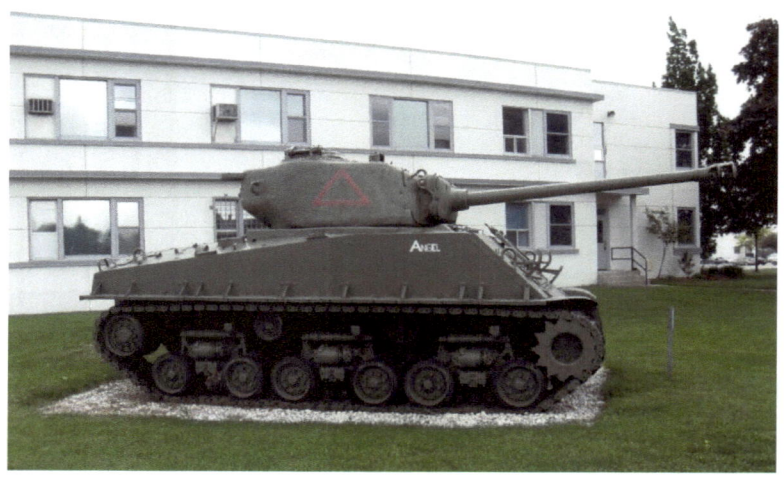

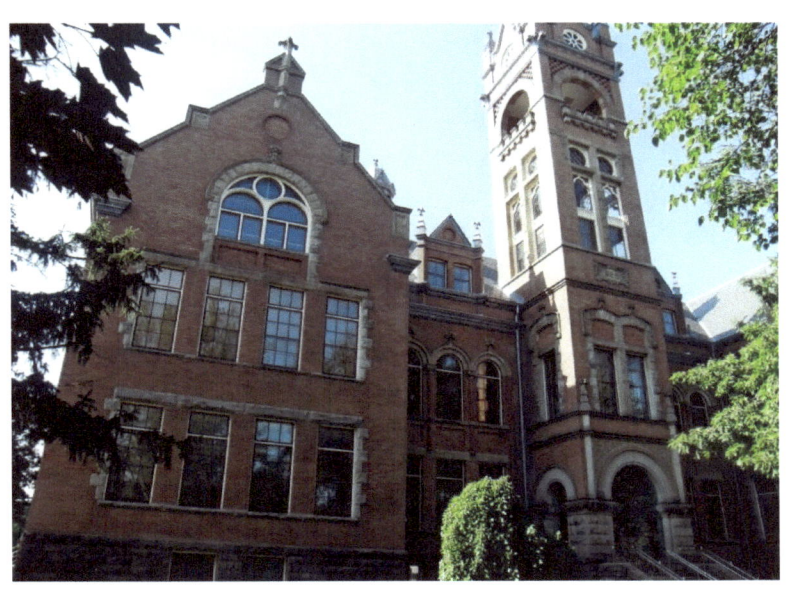

The Normal School
165 Elmwood Avenue East
This 3 storey building was designed in the
High Victorian style in 1898-1899.

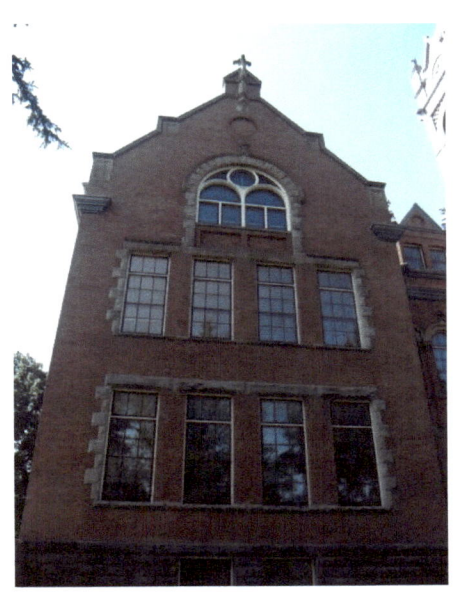

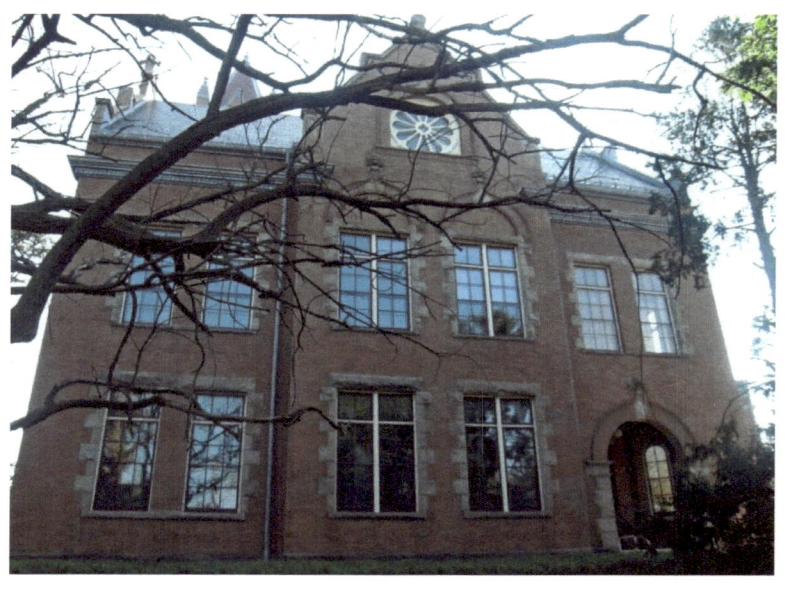

The London Normal School provided
teacher training until 1956.

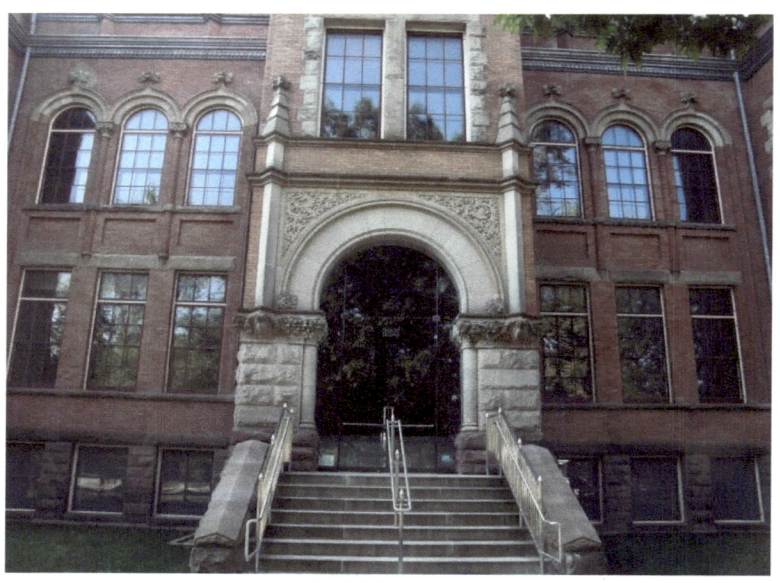

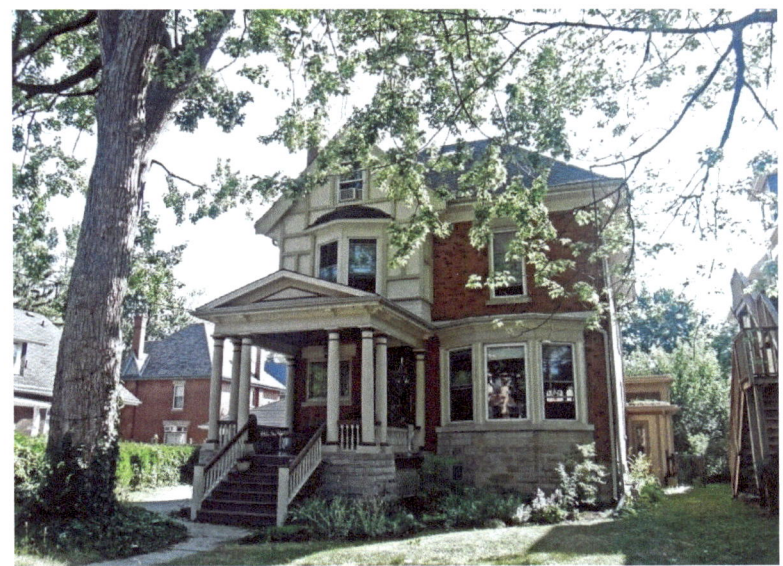

Marley Place – Italianate style – hip roof, pediment above
pillared porch

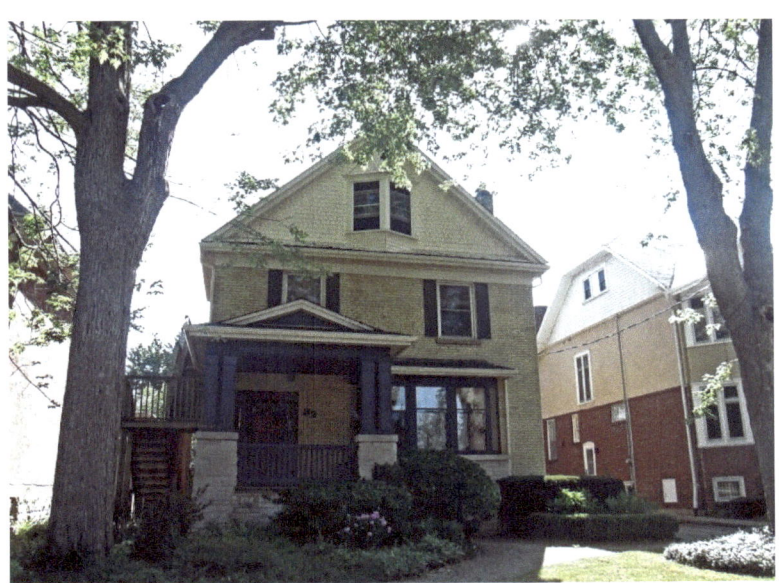

32 Marley Place – Edwardian style

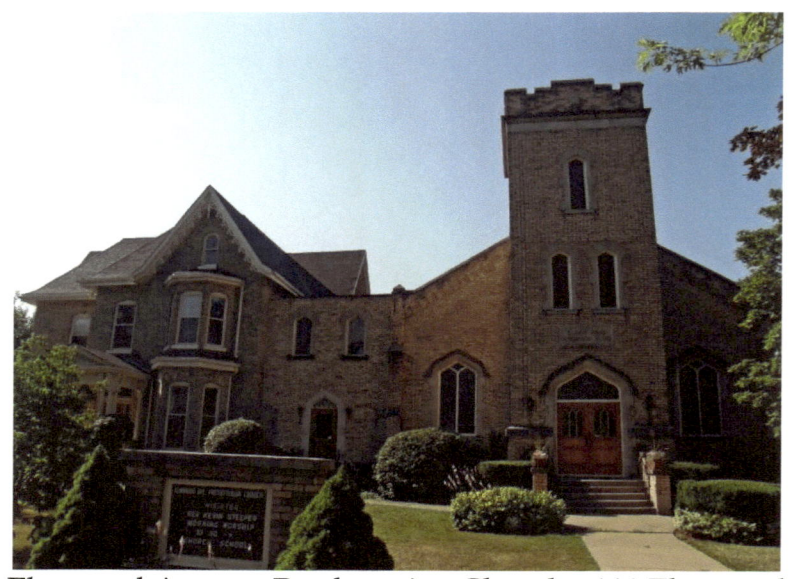

Elmwood Avenue Presbyterian Church - 111 Elmwood Avenue – buttresses, bay windows, Vergeboard trim on gable

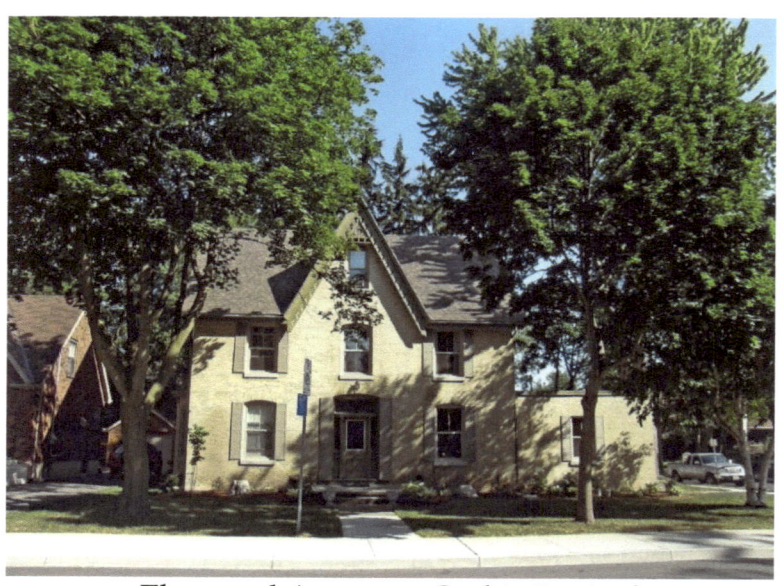

Elmwood Avenue – Gothic Revival

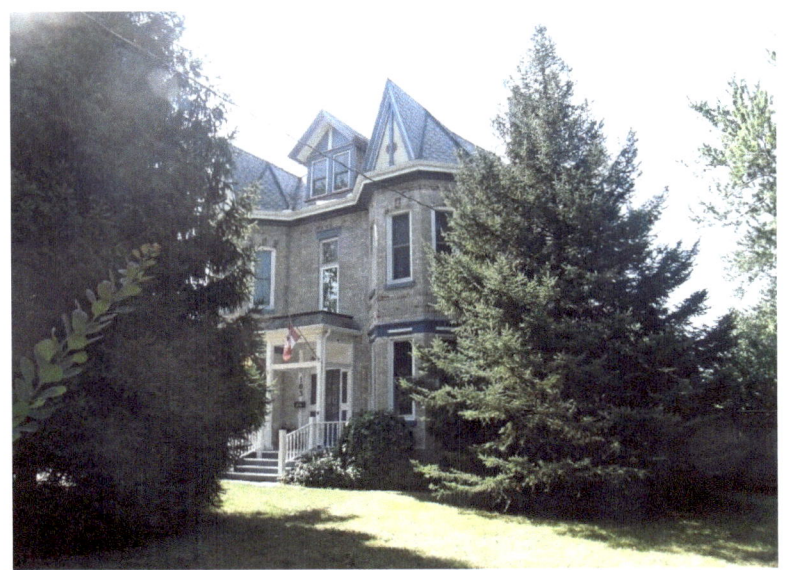

103 Elmwood Avenue – Queen Anne style, dichromatic brickwork

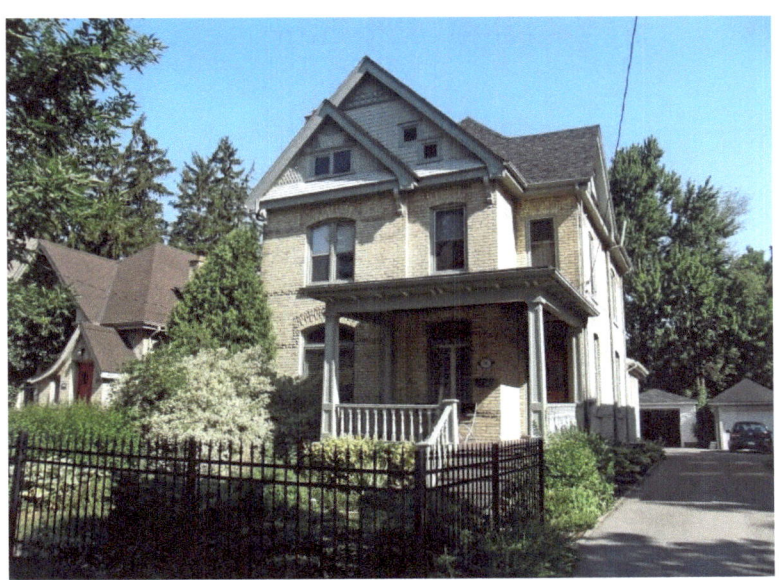

86 Elmwood Avenue –Edwardian style

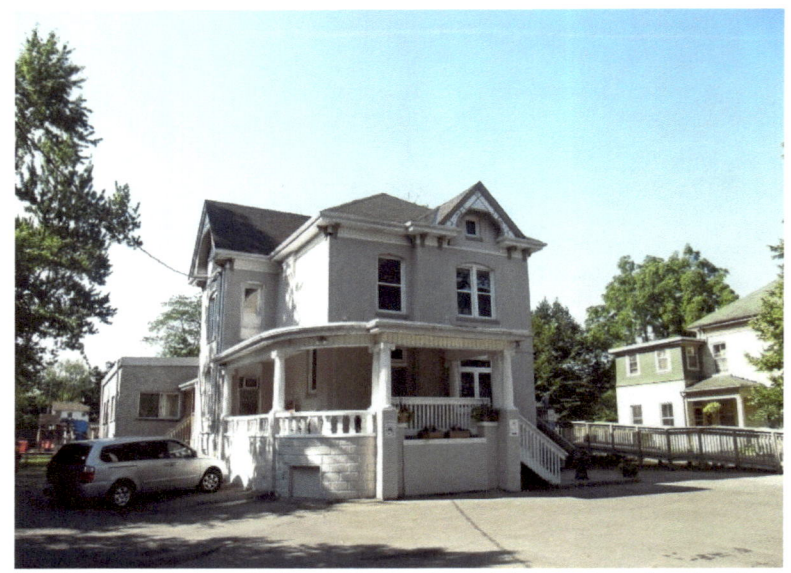

Elmwood Avenue – Italianate style with two-and-a-half storey tower-like bays with vergeboard trim on gables

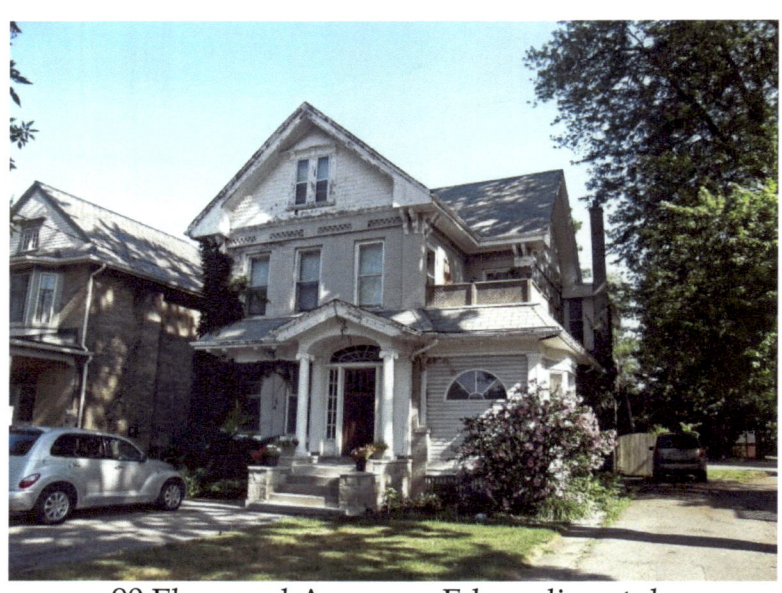

90 Elmwood Avenue – Edwardian style

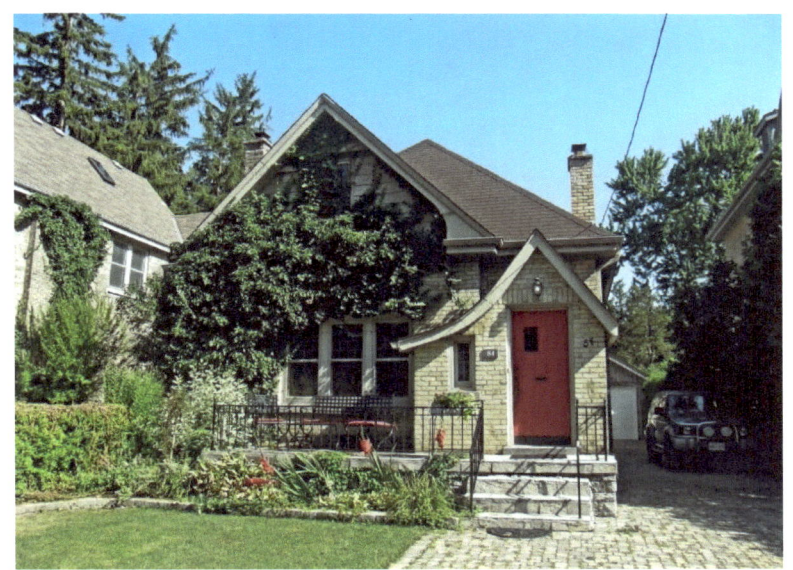

84 Elmwood Avenue

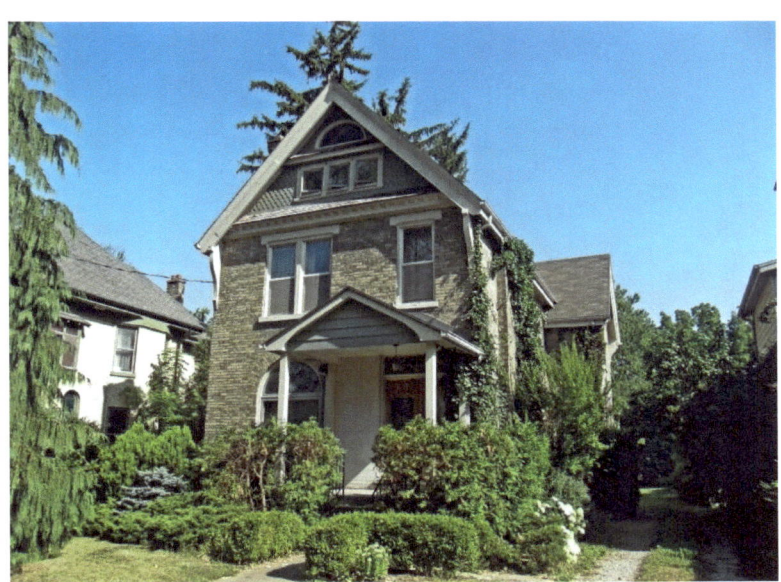

Edwardian style

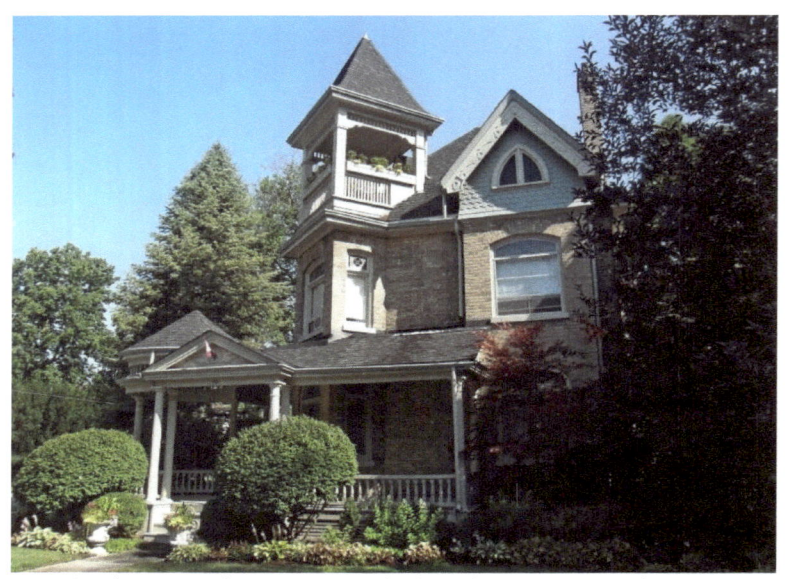

70 Elmwood Avenue – belvedere at top of tower

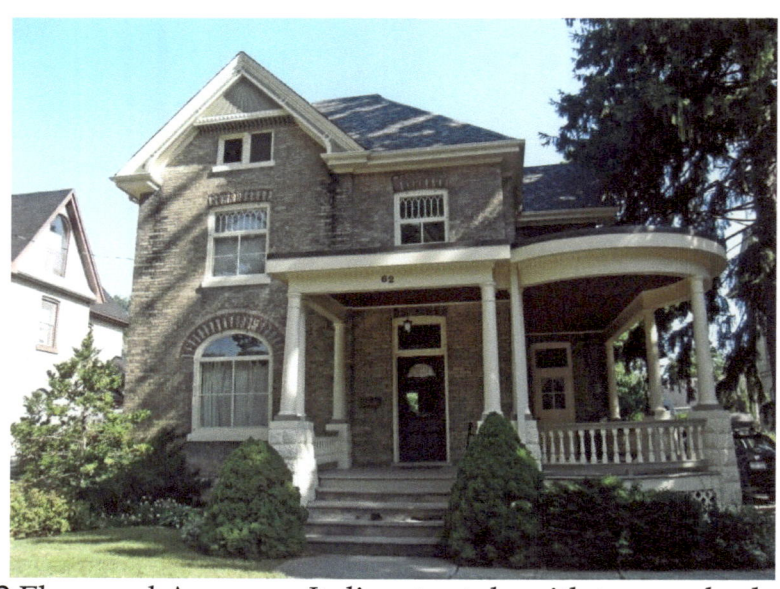

62 Elmwood Avenue – Italianate style with two-and-a-half storey tower-like bay, cornice return on gable

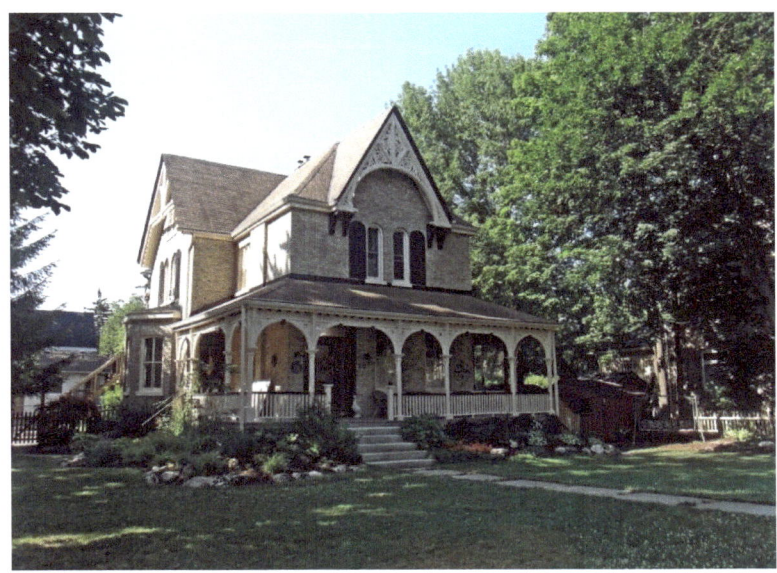

Heritage Property – Gothic Revival in yellow brick

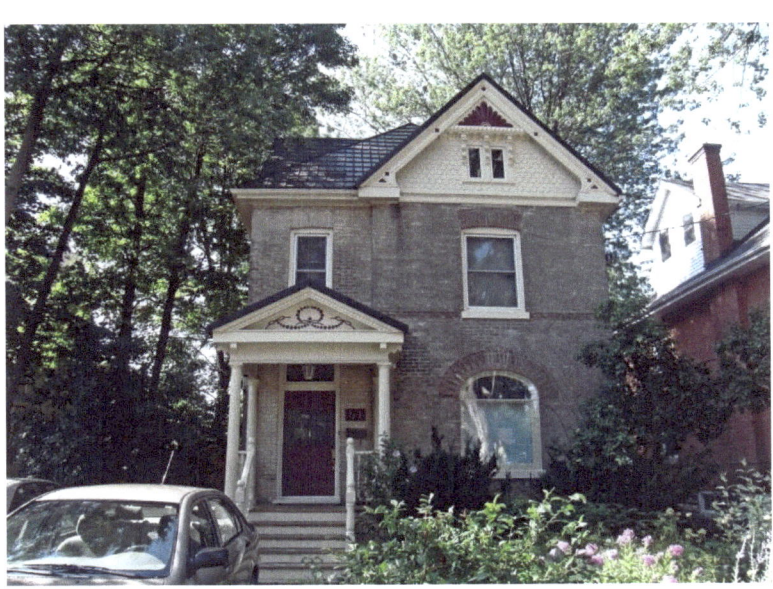

61 Elmwood Avenue

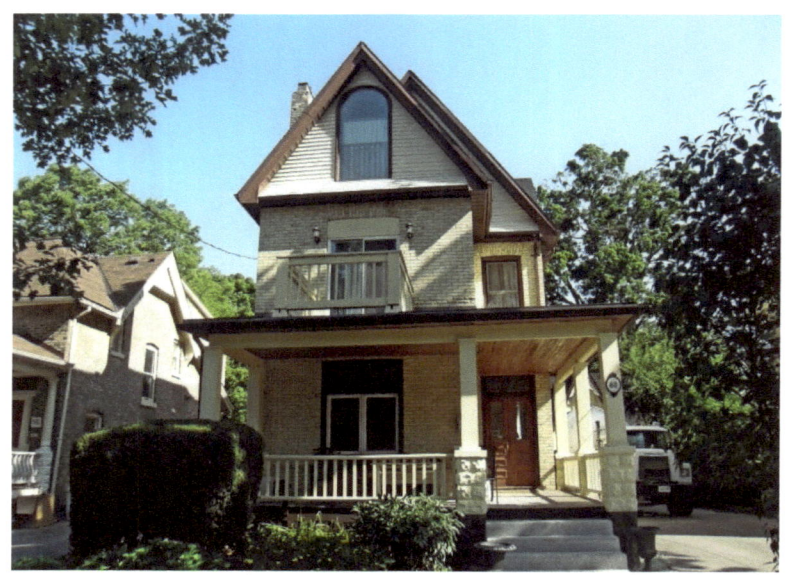

60 Elmwood – Gothic Revival

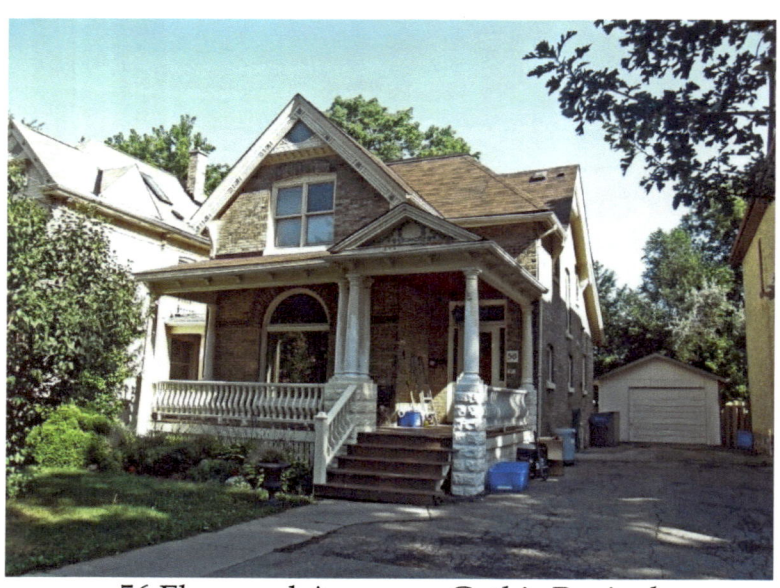

56 Elmwood Avenue – Gothic Revival

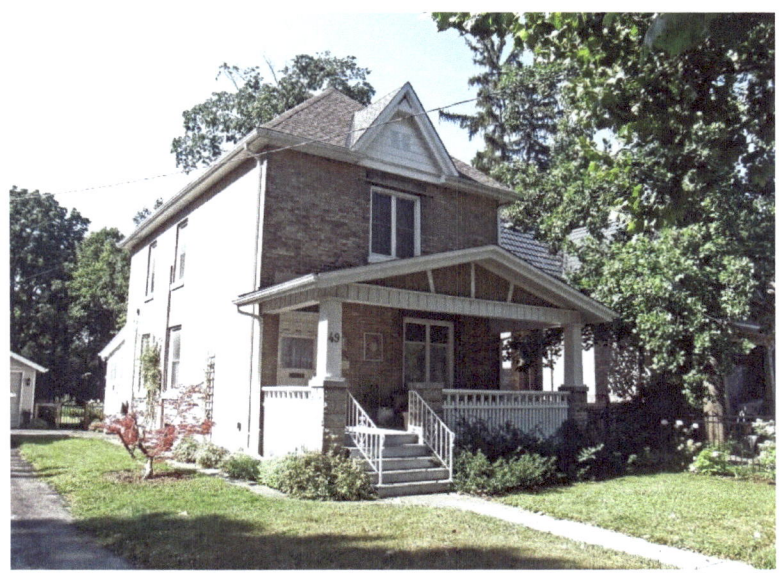

49 Elmwood Avenue – Gothic Revival in yellow brick

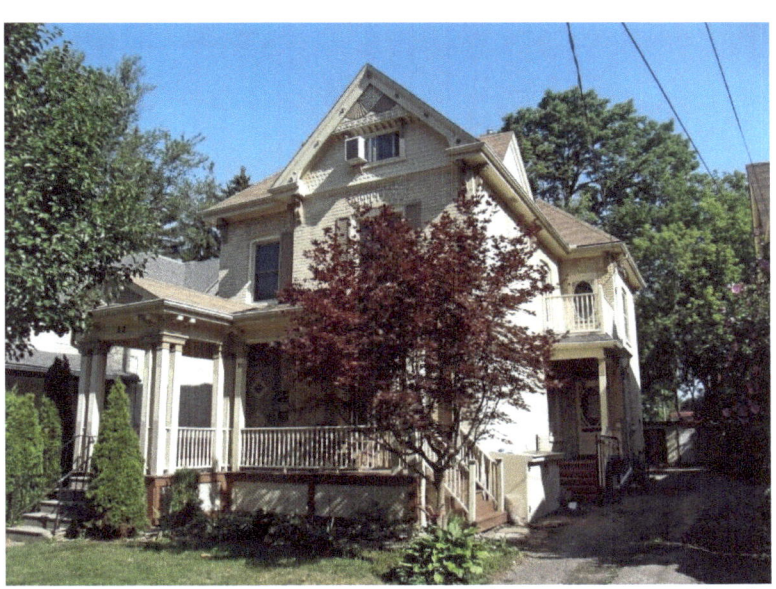

52 Elmwood Avenue – Italianate style with two-and-a-half
storey tower like bay with decorative trim on the gable

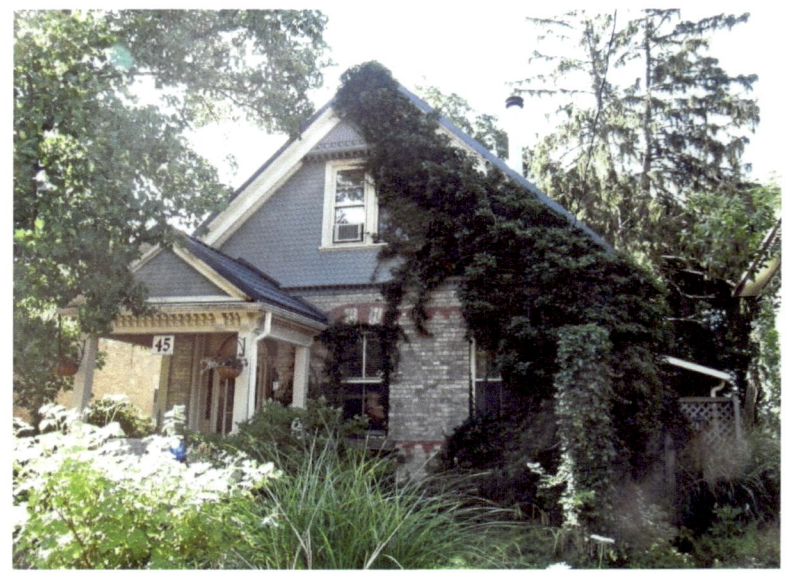

45 Elmwood Avenue – dichromatic brickwork

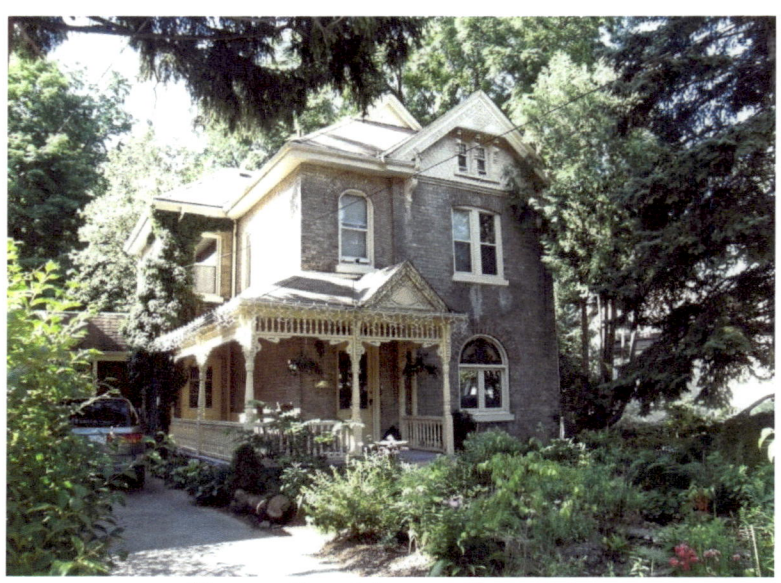

Decorative trim on the gable

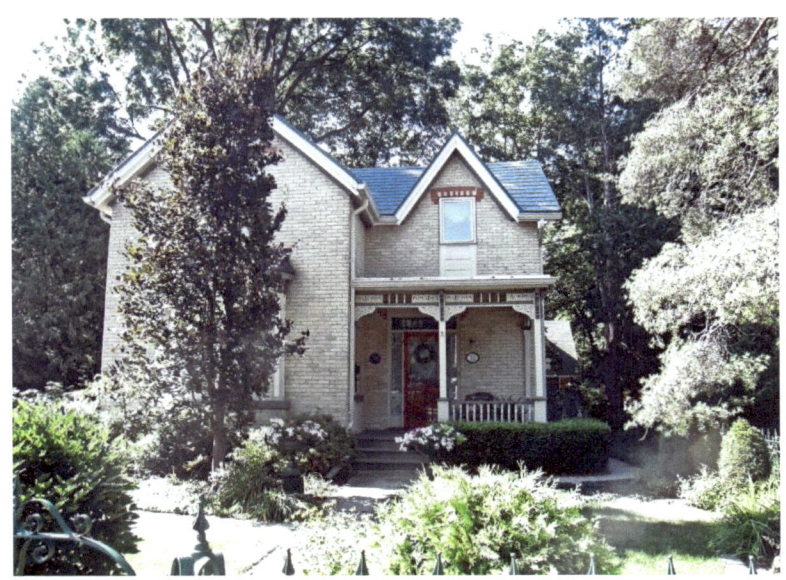

35 Elmwood Avenue

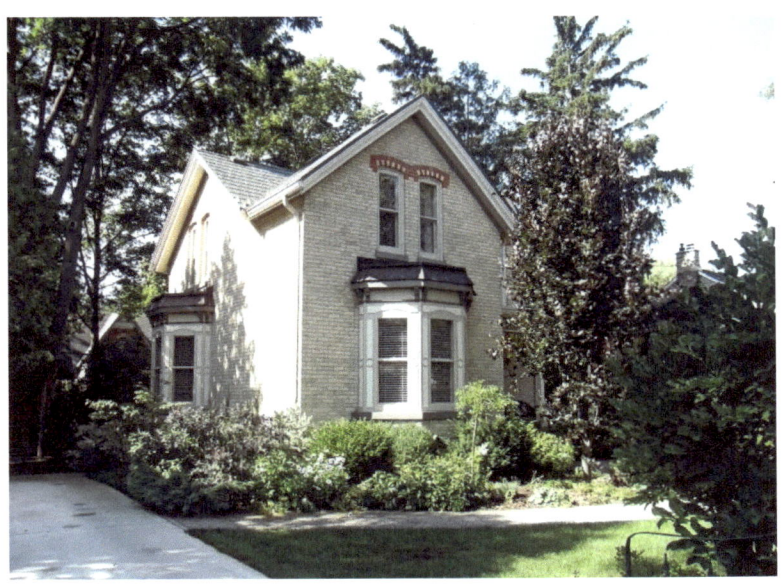

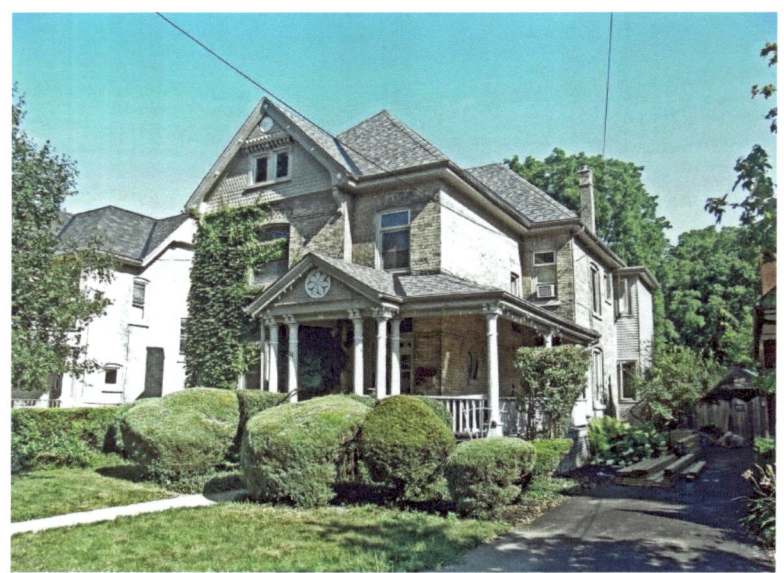

30 Elmwood Avenue – Italianate style, hip roof, decorative work on the gable, pediment with decorative tympanum

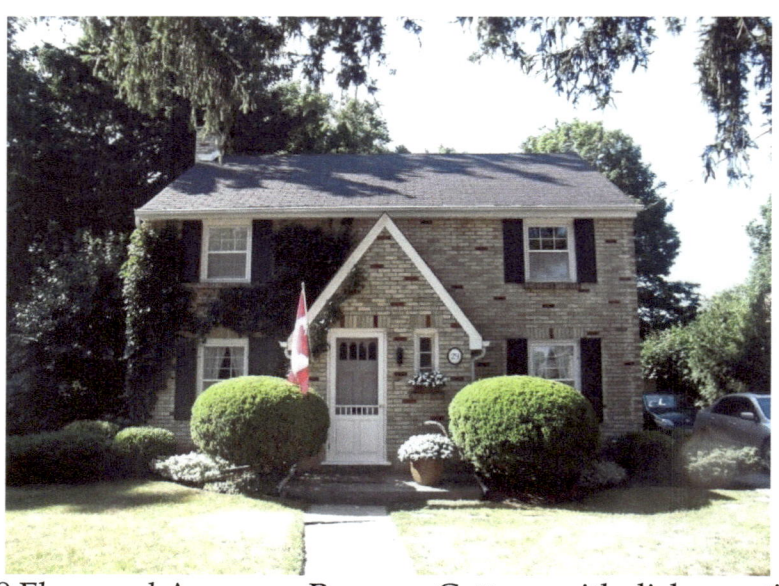

29 Elmwood Avenue – Regency Cottage with dichromatic brickwork using two colours of brick

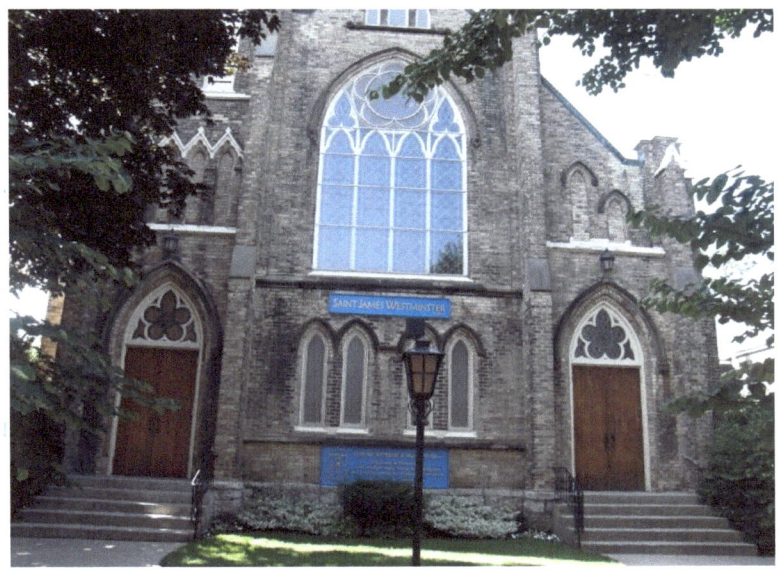

Saint James Wesminster Anglican Church
115 Askin Street
The first church was opened here in 1873.

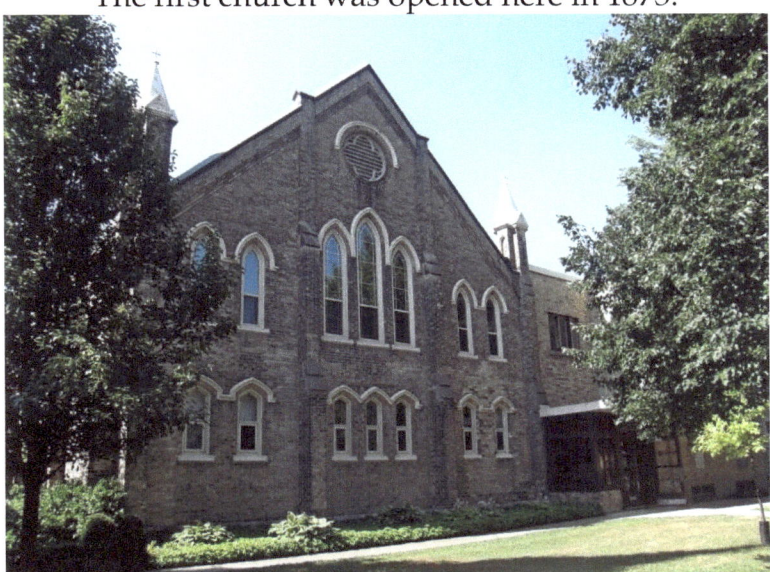

Lancet windows

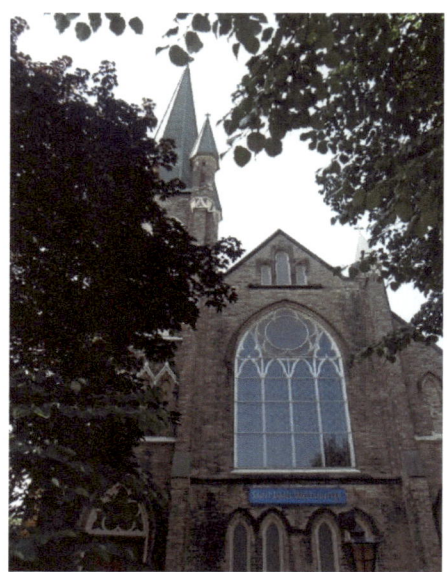

Gothic Revival

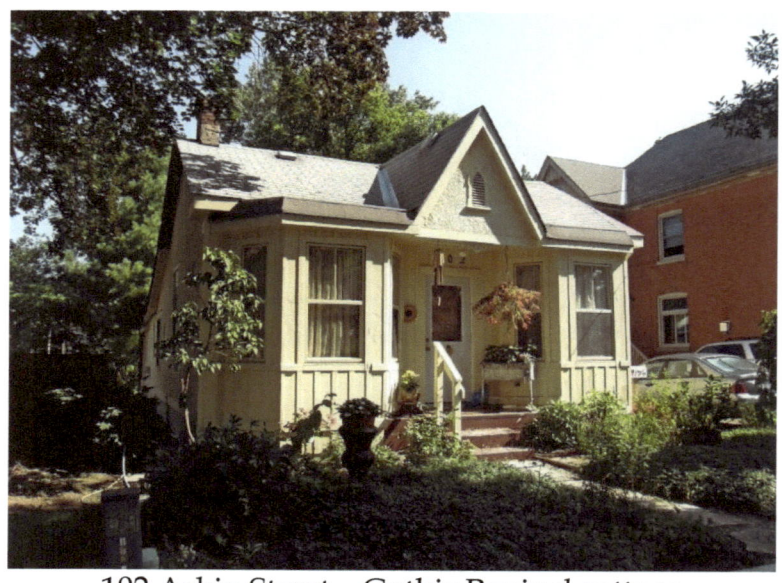

102 Askin Street – Gothic Revival cottage

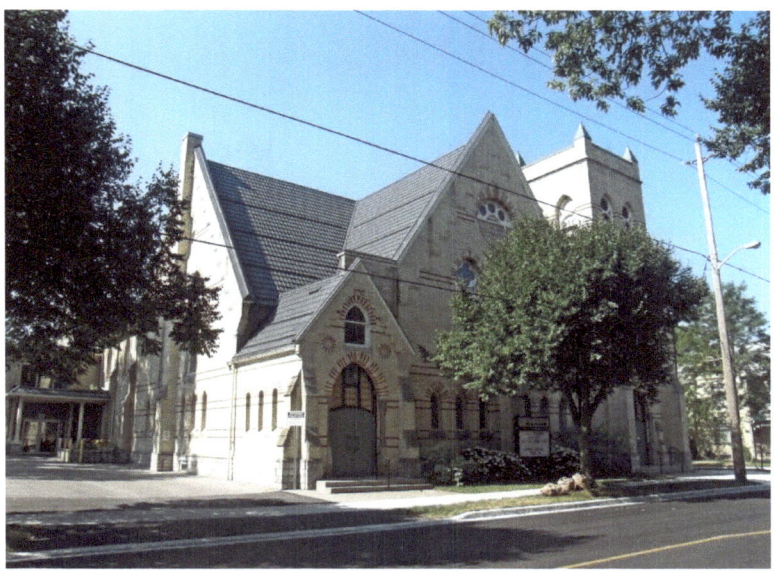

Wesley-Knox United Church - 91 Askin Street
Founded in 1874 as New Brighton Methodist Church.
It later became Askin Street Methodist Church, and with
Church union in 1925 it became Wesley United Church.
In 1972 Knox and Wesley United Churches combined.

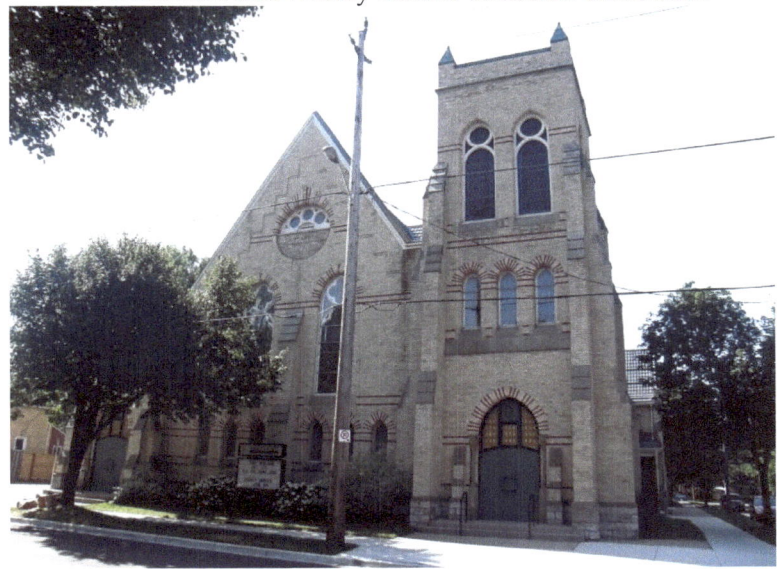

Dichromatic brickwork

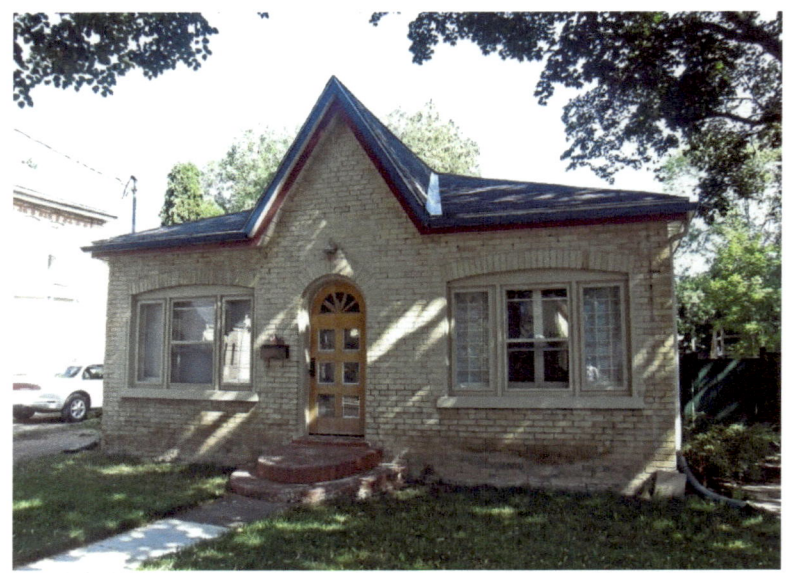

96 Askin Street – Gothic Cottage in yellow brick

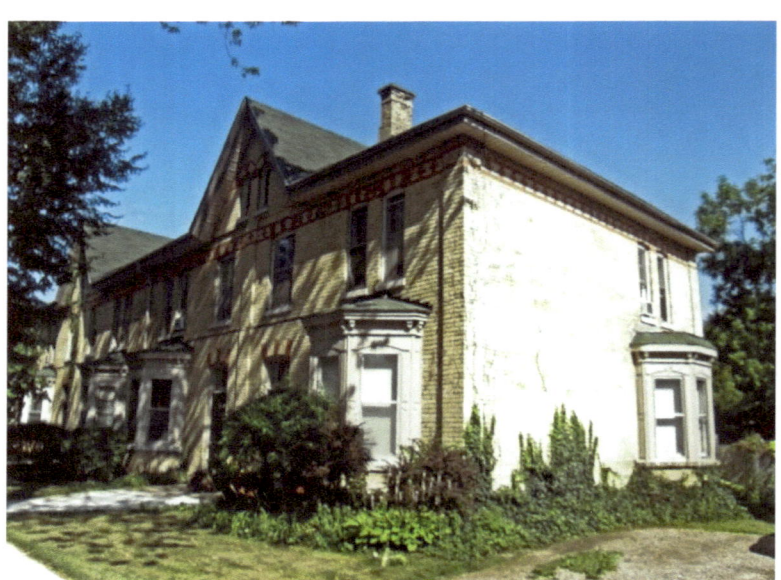

Gothic Revival – dichromatic brickwork – bay windows

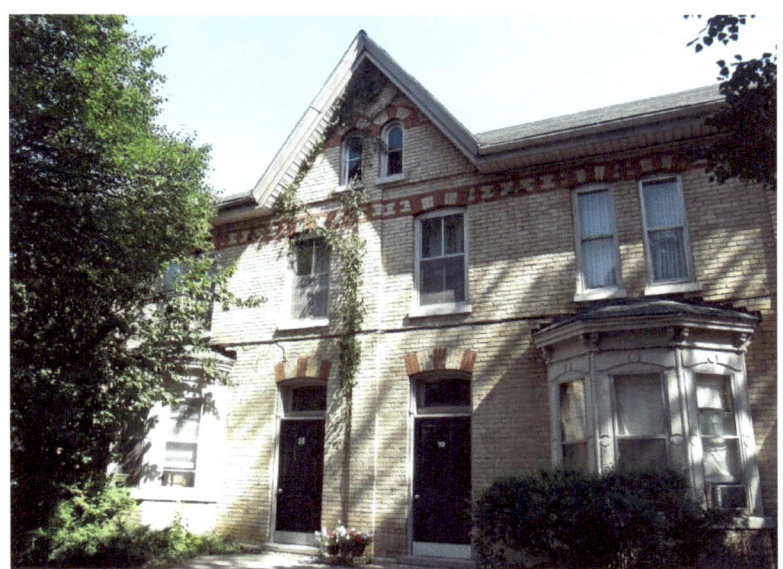

88, 90 Askin Street – Gothic Revival - decorative dichromatic brickwork, bay window

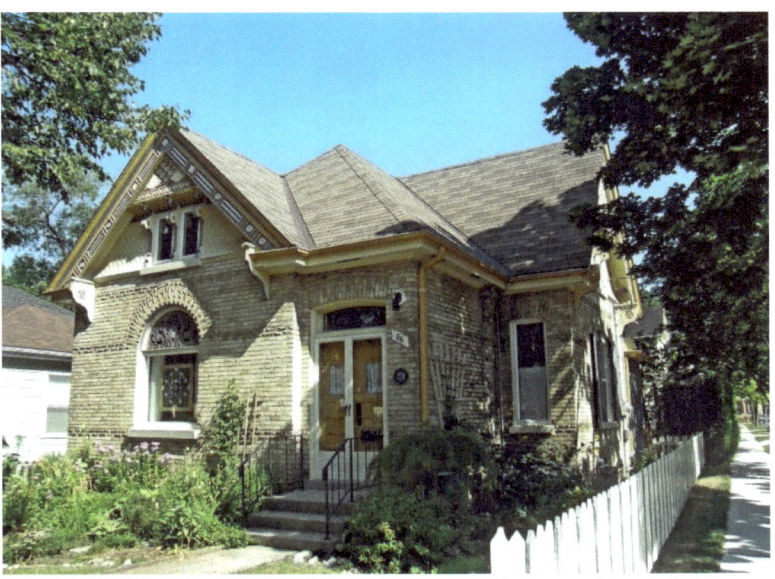

86 Askin Street – Verge board trim on the gables

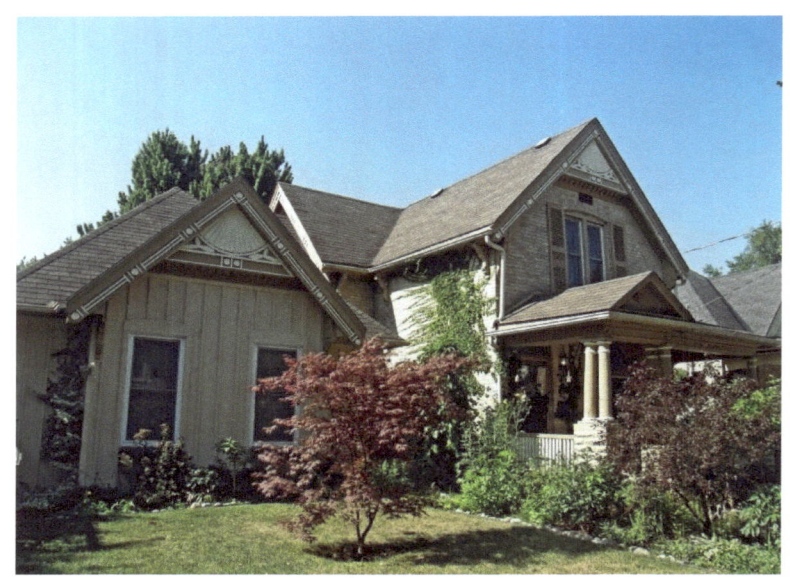

Gothic Revival

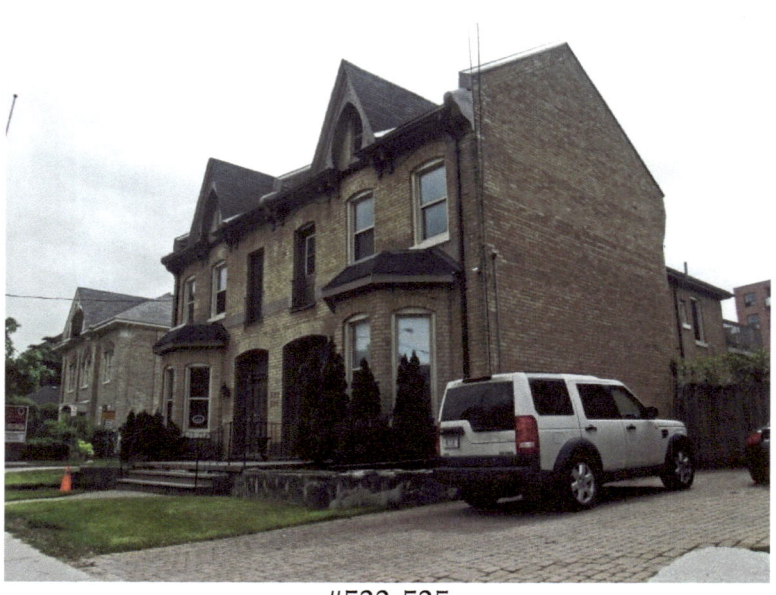

#533-535

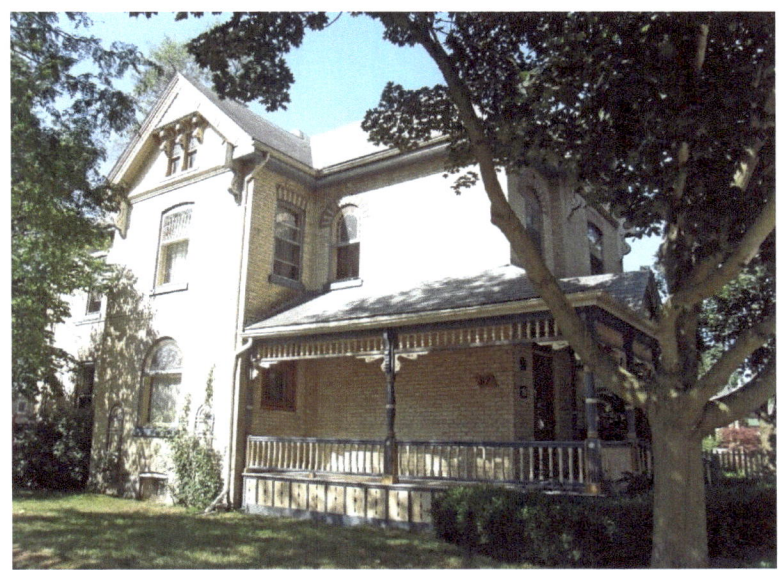

87 Askin Street – Italianate style with two-and-a-half storey tower-like bay, arched window voussoirs in contrasting color, cornice brackets

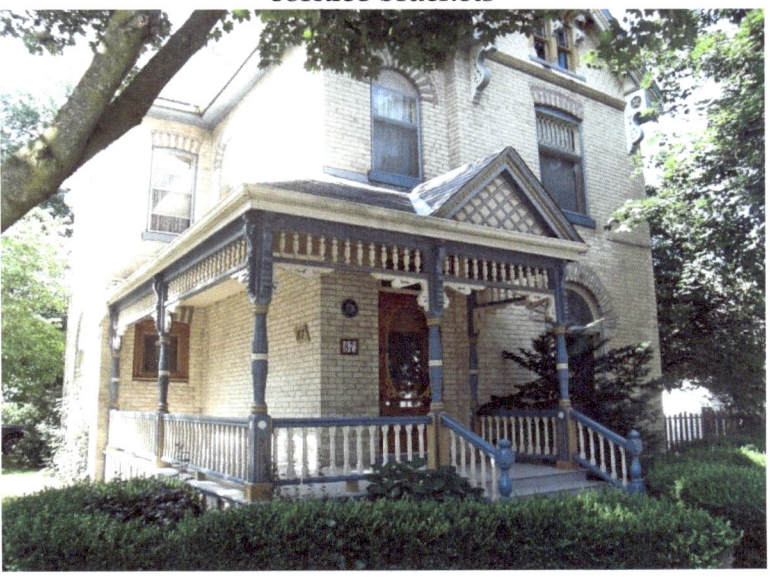

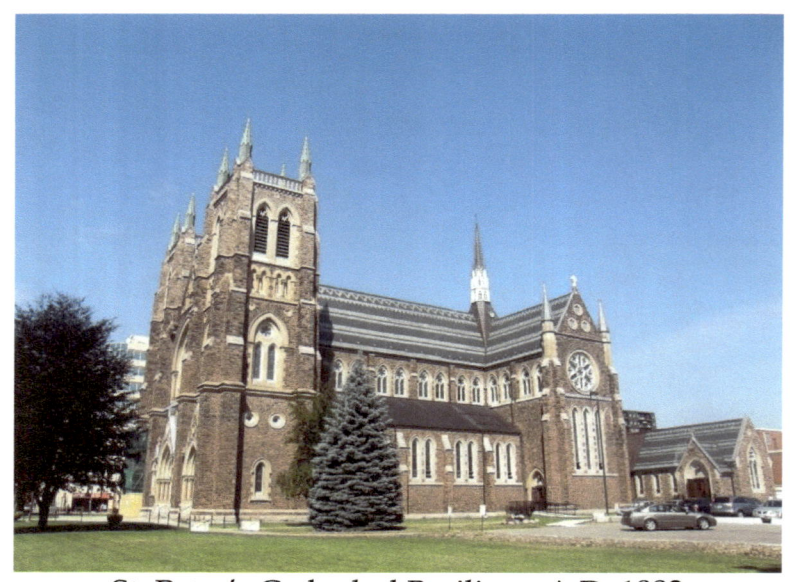

St. Peter's Cathedral Basilica – A.D. 1882
533 Clarence Street – rose window, lancet windows

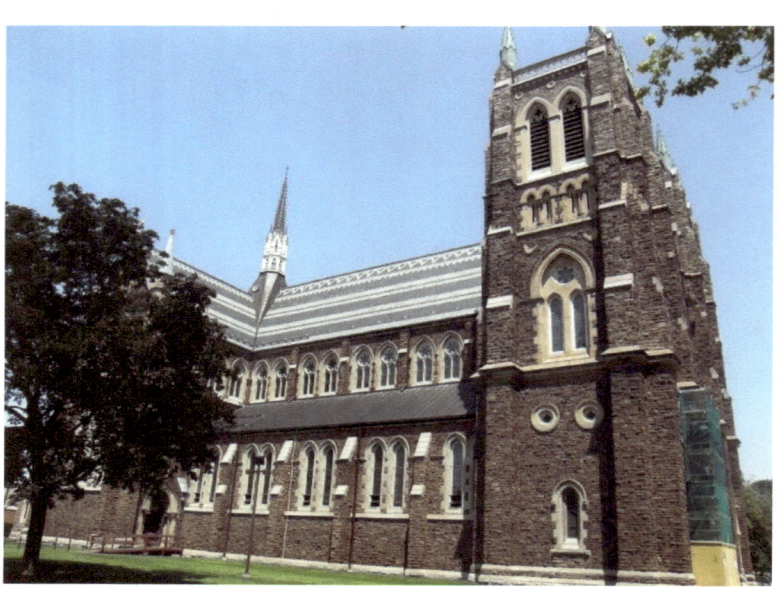

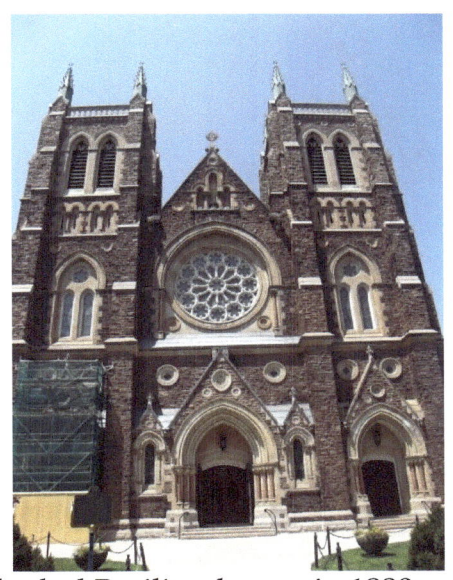

St. Peter's Cathedral Basilica, begun in 1880 and dedicated in 1885, is in the 13th Century French Gothic style. Some of its notable features are the massive bell towers, high transepts, an imposing sanctuary, and the rose window built in Innsbruck, Austria.

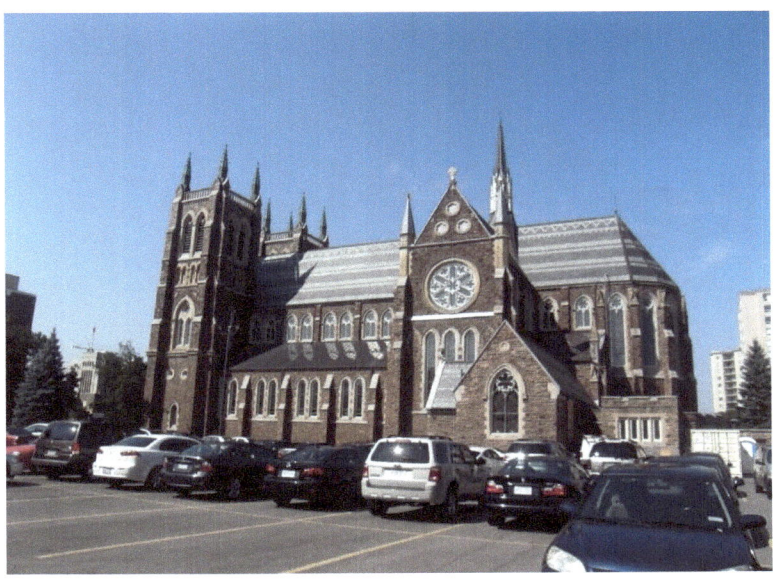

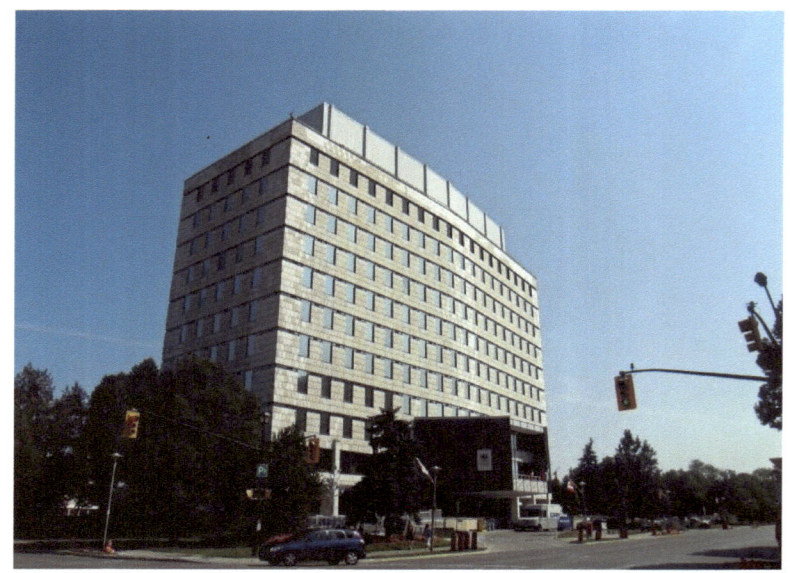

London City Hall – Dufferin Street

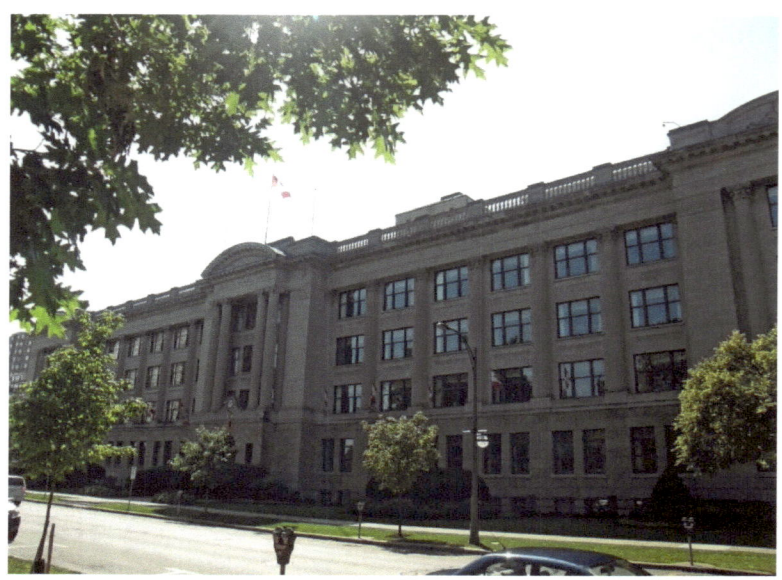

London Life Insurance Company – founded in 1874
255 Dufferin Avenue – built in 1927 – neoclassical design

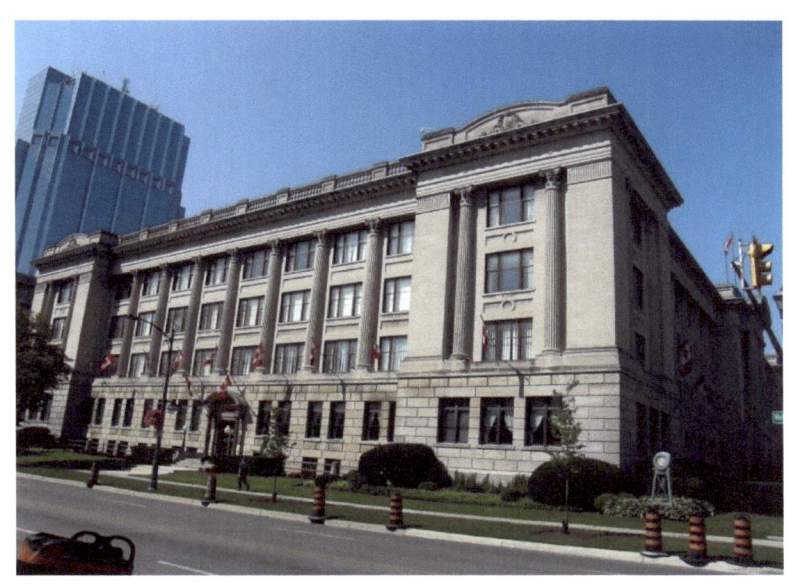

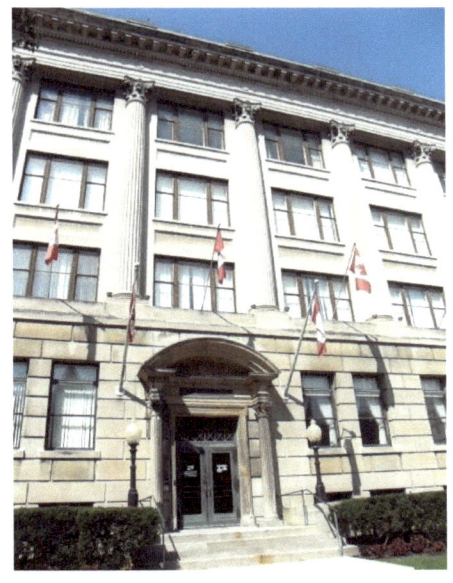

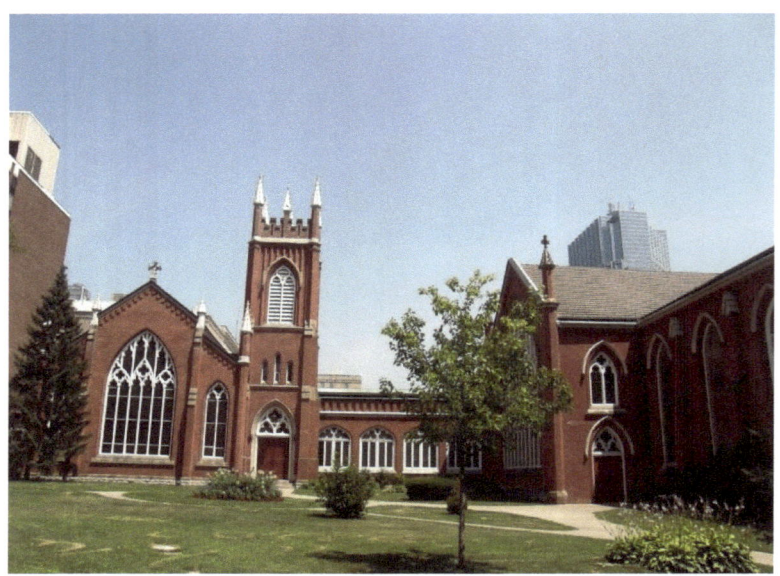

The nave and tower of St. Paul's Anglican Cathedral were designed in the English Gothic Revival style. Previously services were held in a wooden structure on this site from 1834 until it was destroyed by fire in 1844.

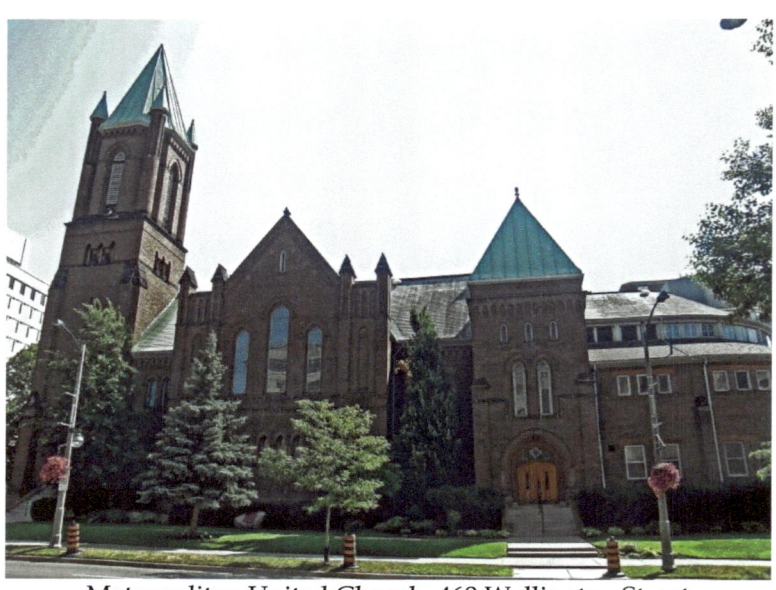

Metropolitan United Church, 468 Wellington Street
Corner stone laid in 1852, destroyed by fire February 2, 1895,
this stone laid July 30, 1895

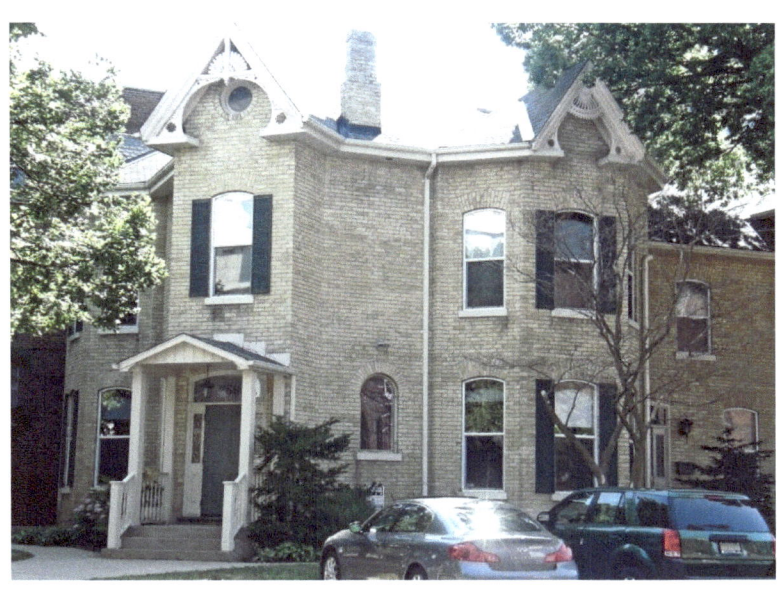

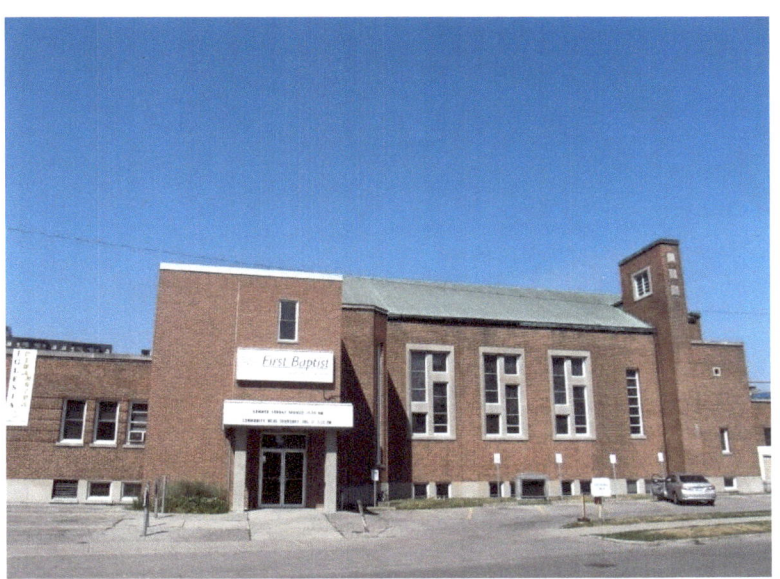

First Baptist Church on the Park
568 Richmond Street

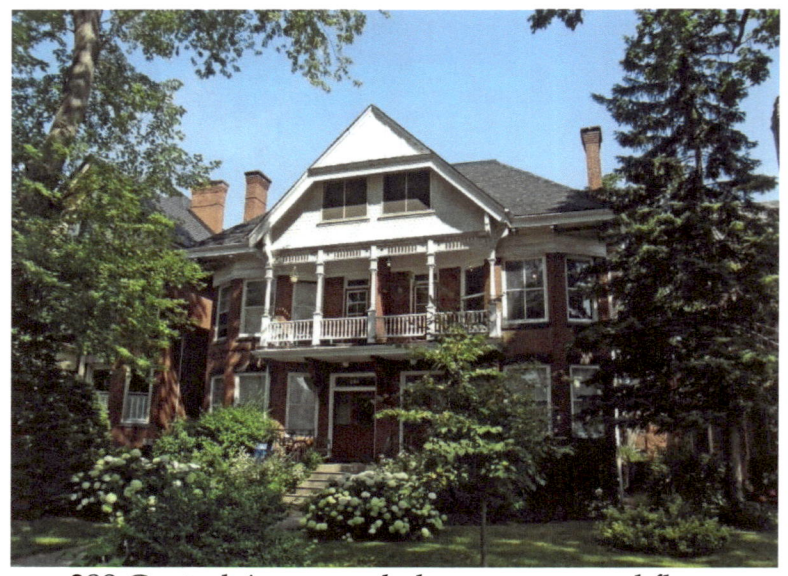

288 Central Avenue – balcony on second floor

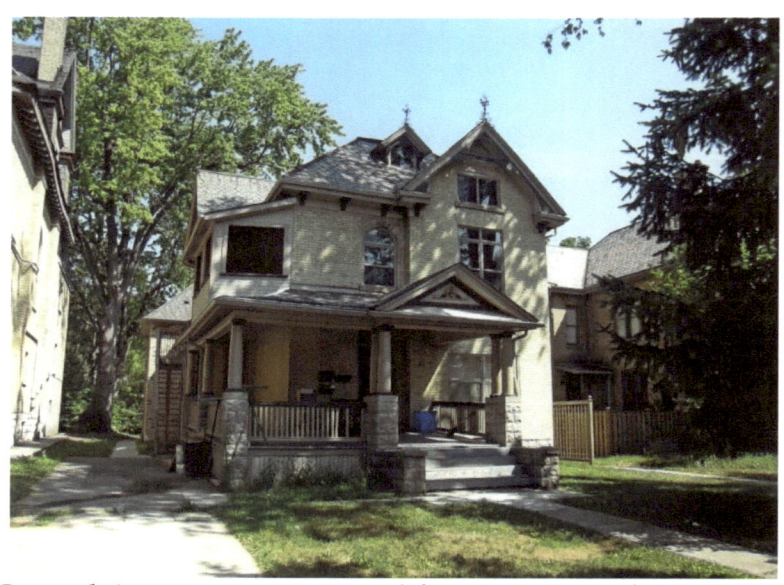

Central Avenue - ornamental finials on top of the gables, cornice return, dormer in the attic

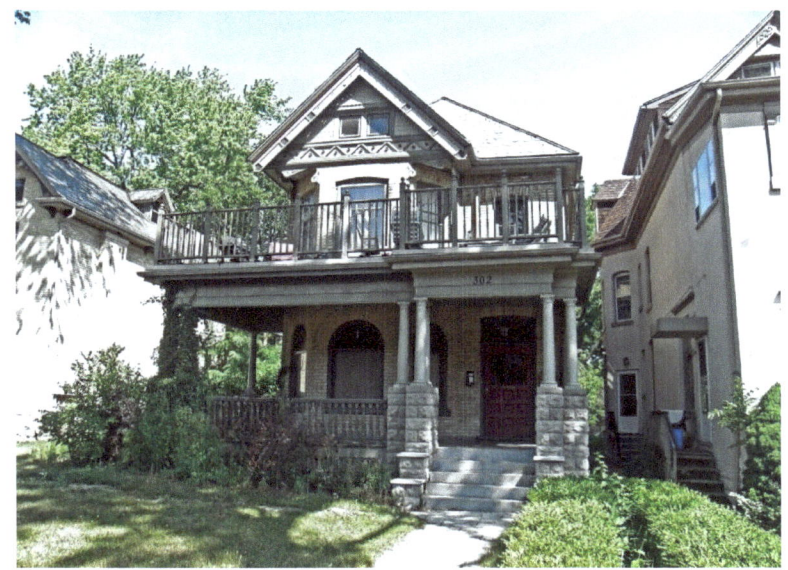

302 Central Avenue – decorative gable, wrap-around balcony
on second floor

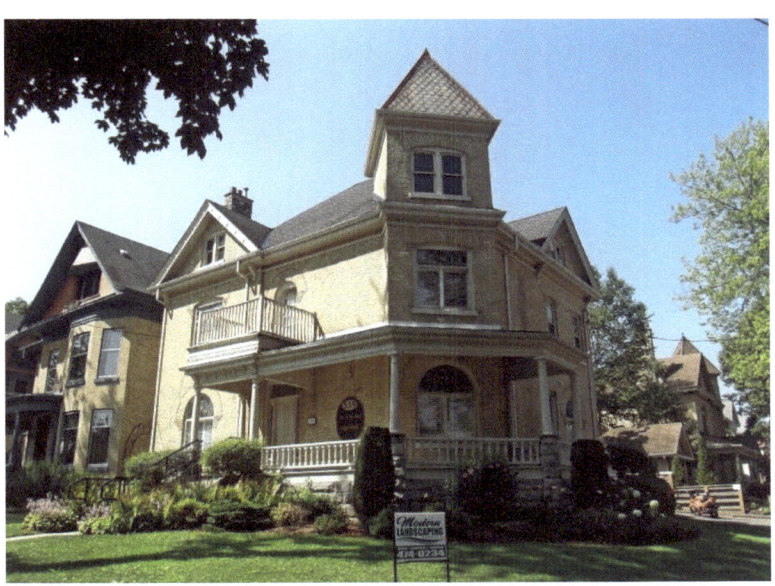

559 Waterloo Street

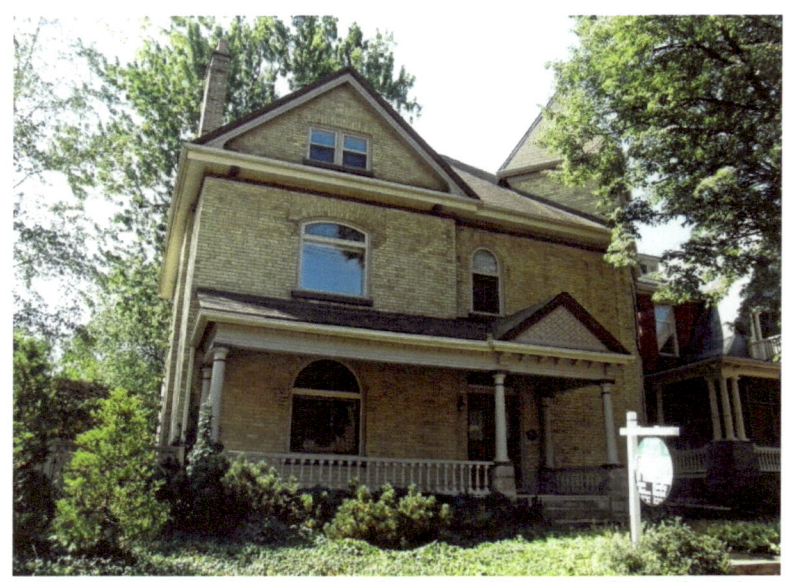

Heritage property - made out of local yellow brick

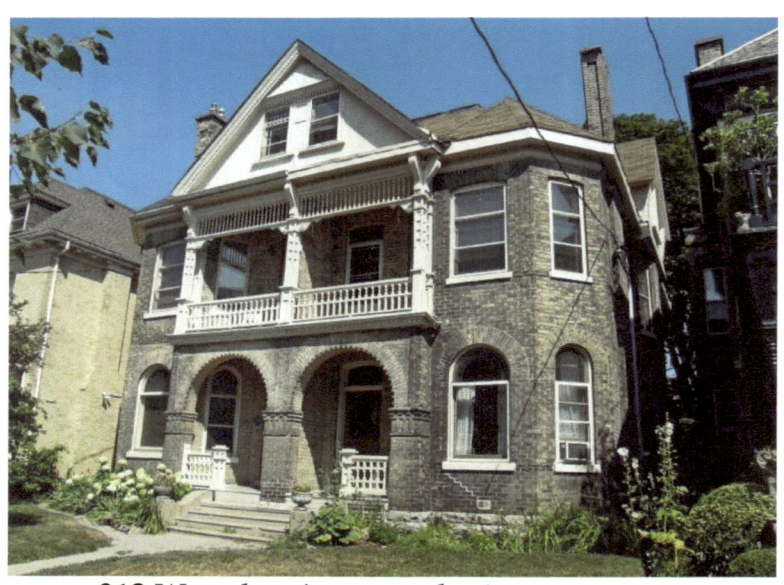

312 Waterloo Avenue – heritage property

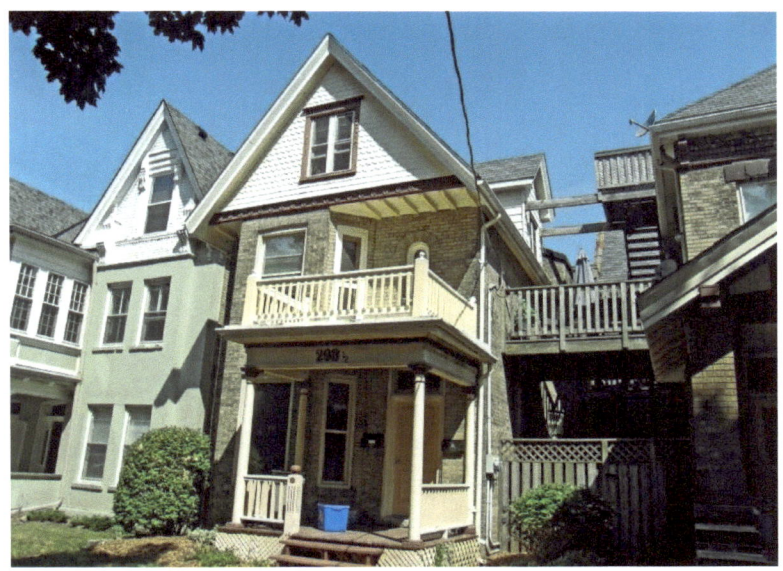

298½ Waterloo Avenue – Edwardian style

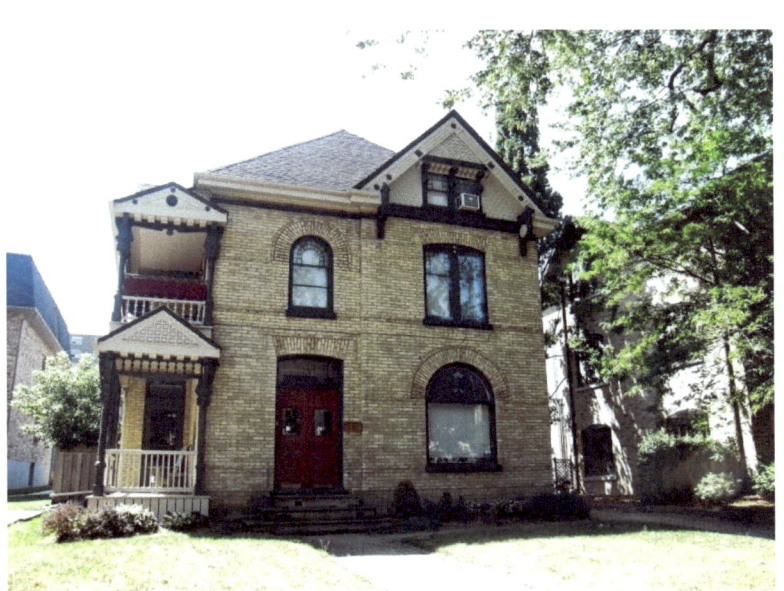

297 Waterloo Avenue – decorative window voussoirs

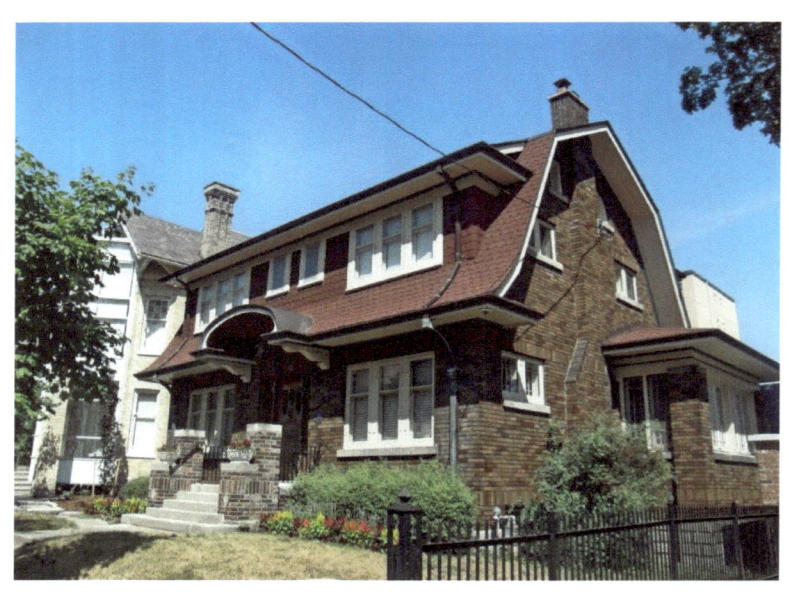

Heritage property – Gothic Revival

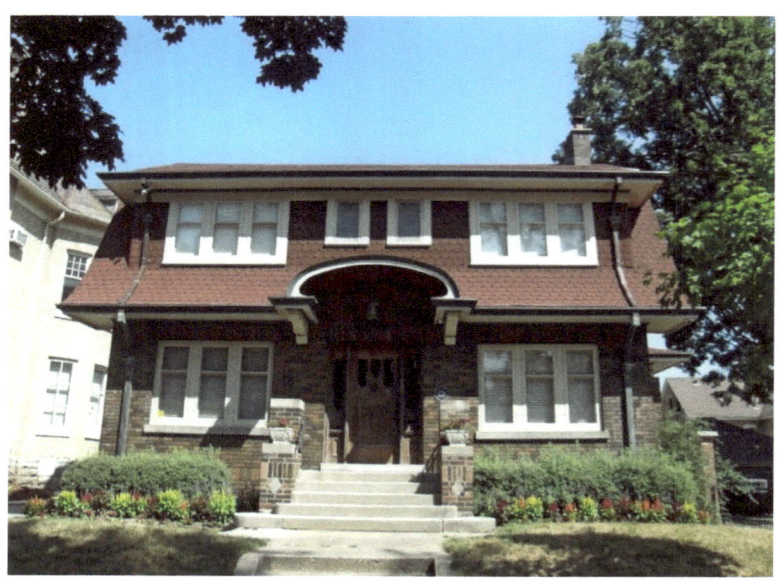

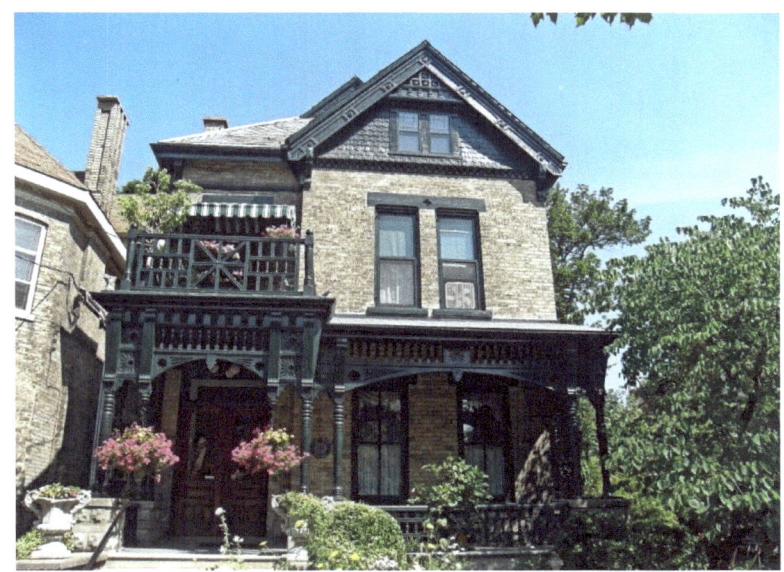

Heritage property

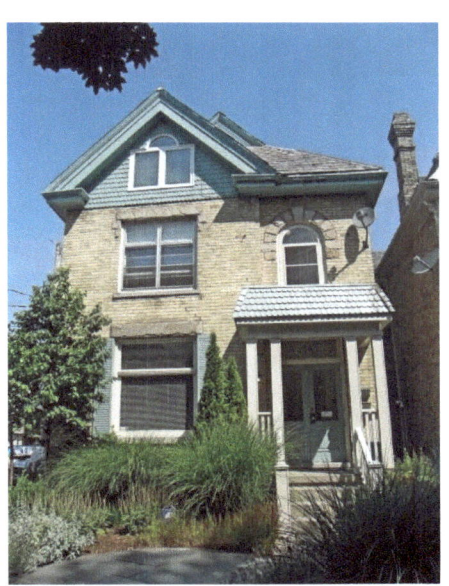

#294 – Gothic Revival

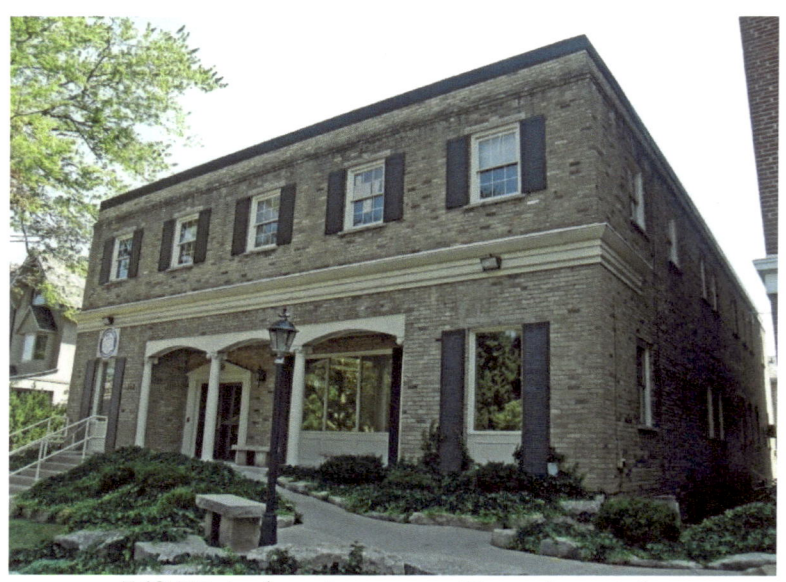

562 Waterloo Avenue – Georgian style

University of Western Ontario

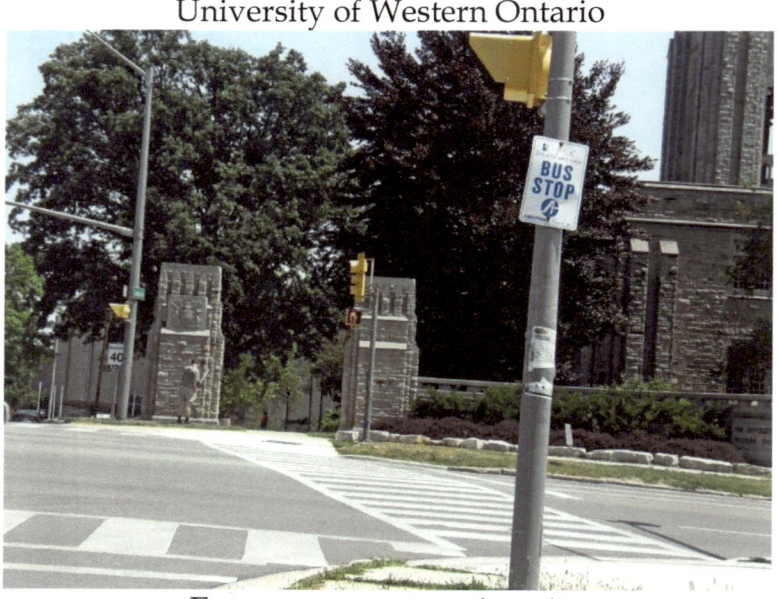

Entrance gates to university

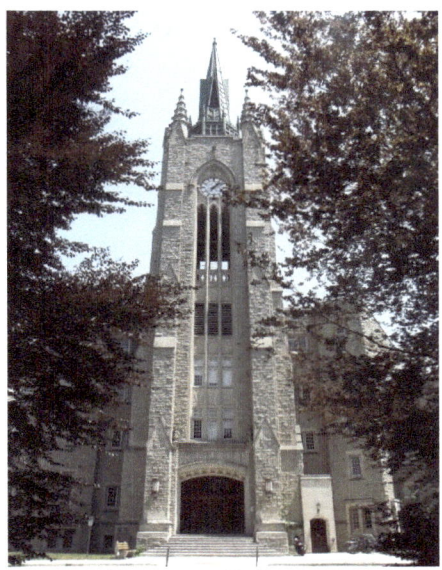

Middlesex College – 1959 – Neo-Gothic style

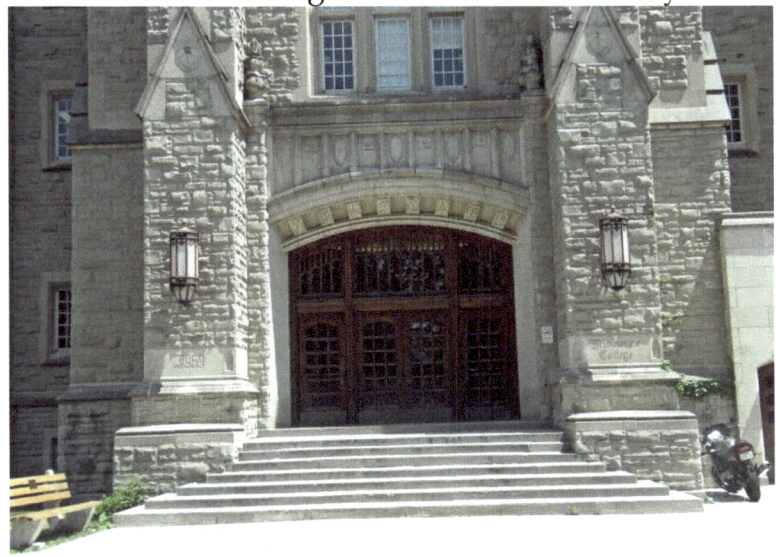

Buttresses, mullions in the windows of the doors with the upper ones more decorative with ogee arches; shields and quatrefoils above the doorway arch

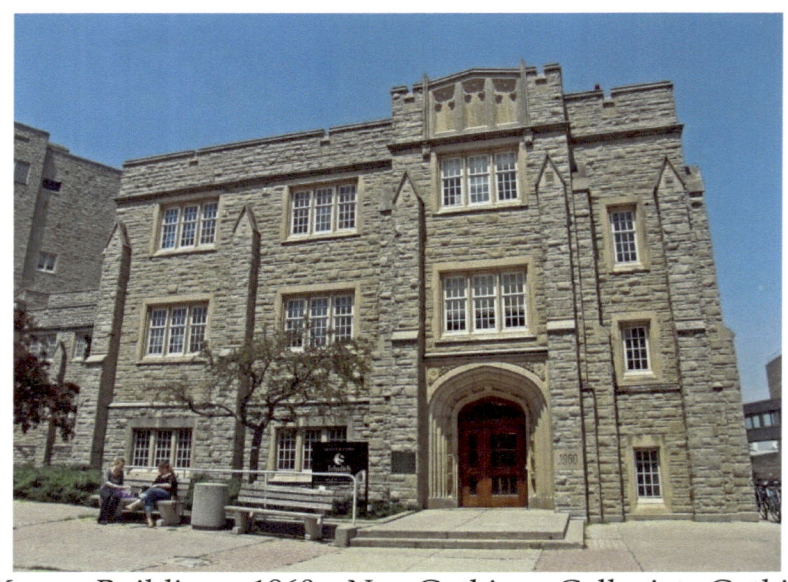

Kresge Building – 1960 – Neo-Gothic or Collegiate Gothic style – buttresses, battlementing; the archway has a beautifully carved reveal and spandrels

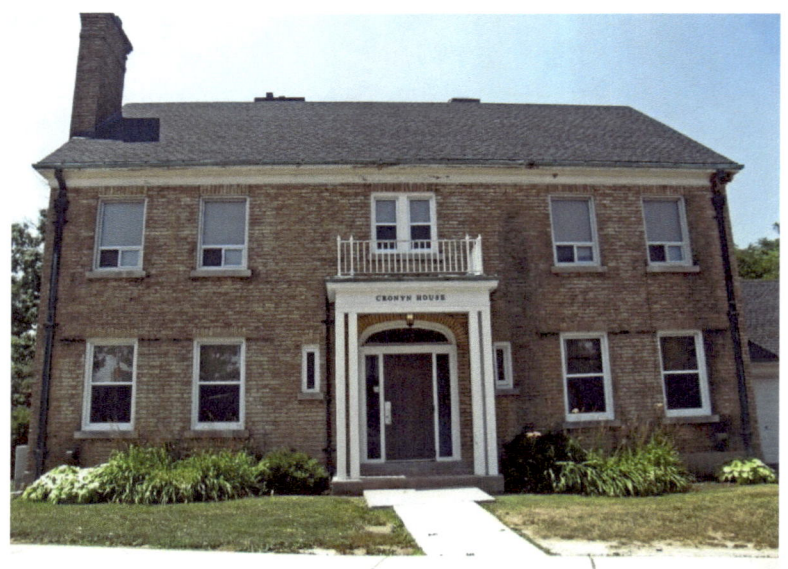

Cronyn House

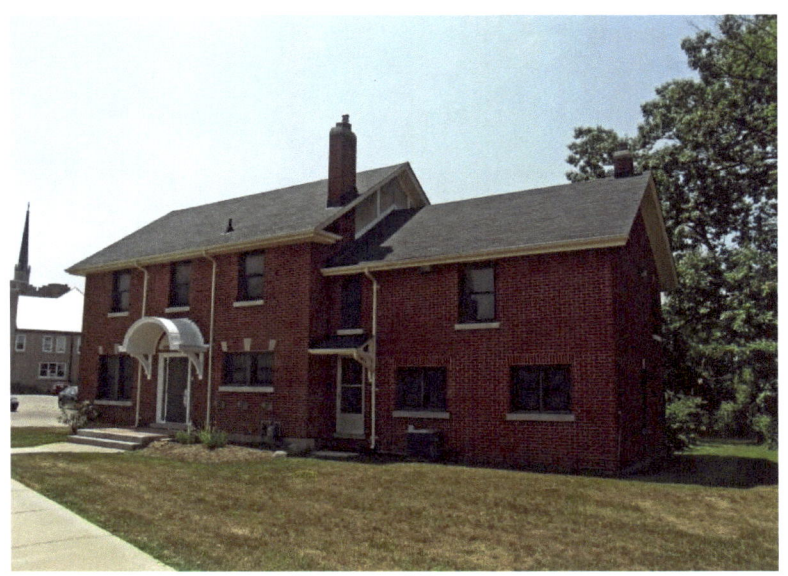

Benson House

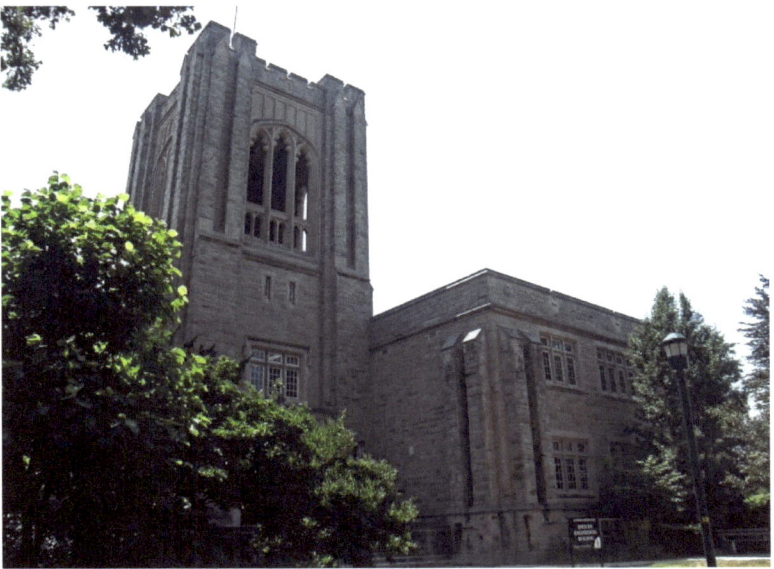

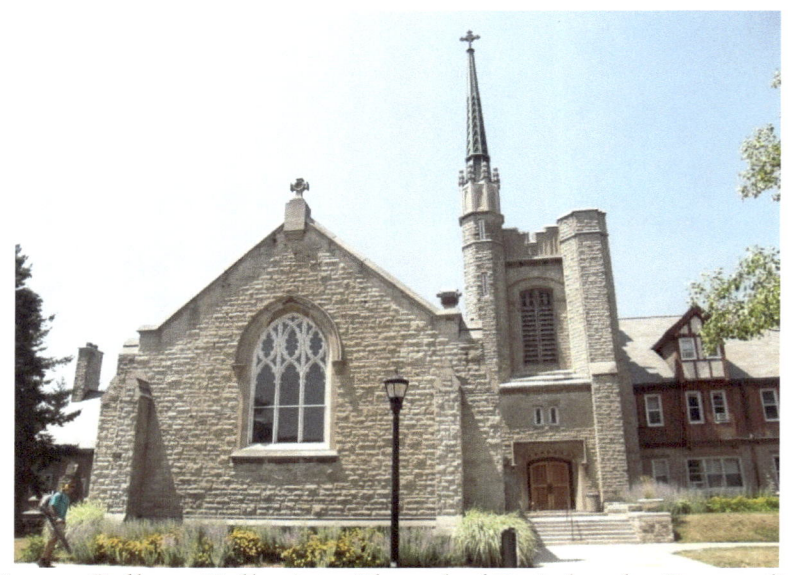

Huron College Collegiate Chapel of St. John the Evangelist (Anglican)

Huron College was founded in 1863 by the Right Reverend Benjamin Cronyn elected in 1857 as the first Anglican Bishop of Huron. He saw the need for a theological school and institution for advanced studies for the people in the growing community. The professors and alumni of this college established the Western University of London, founded in 1878 and affiliated with Huron in 1881.

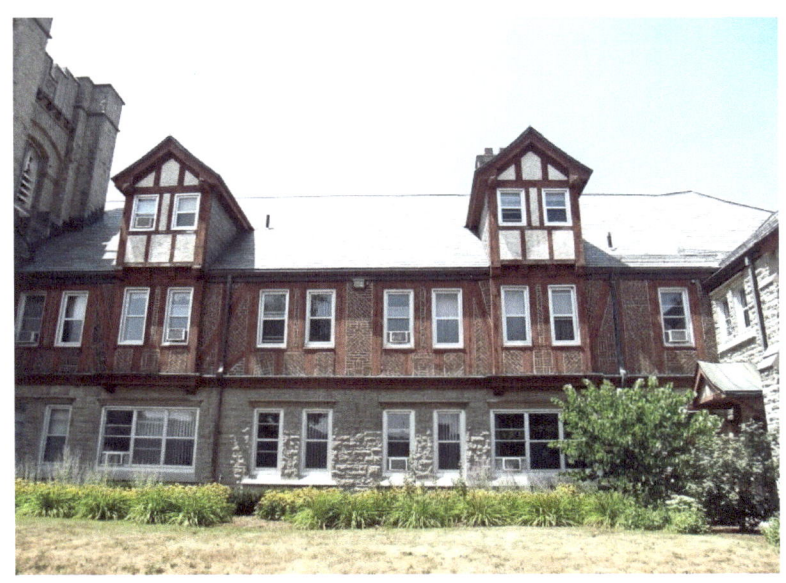

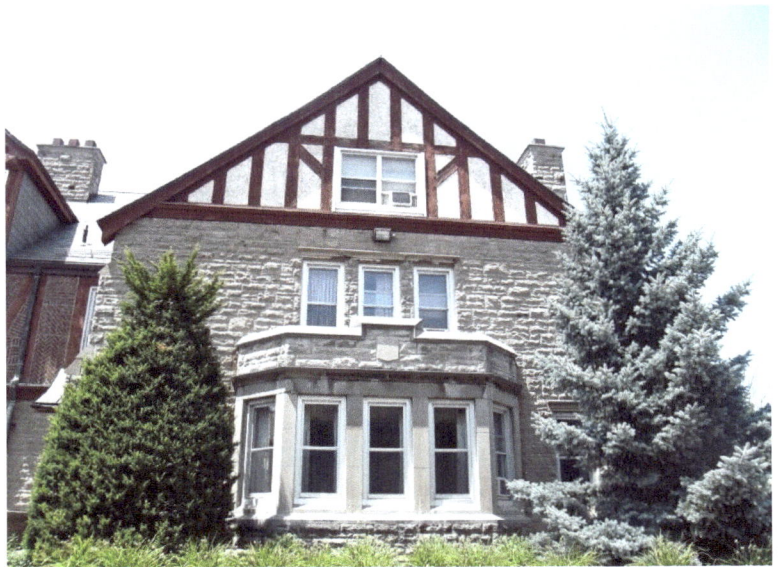

Tudor style in gable

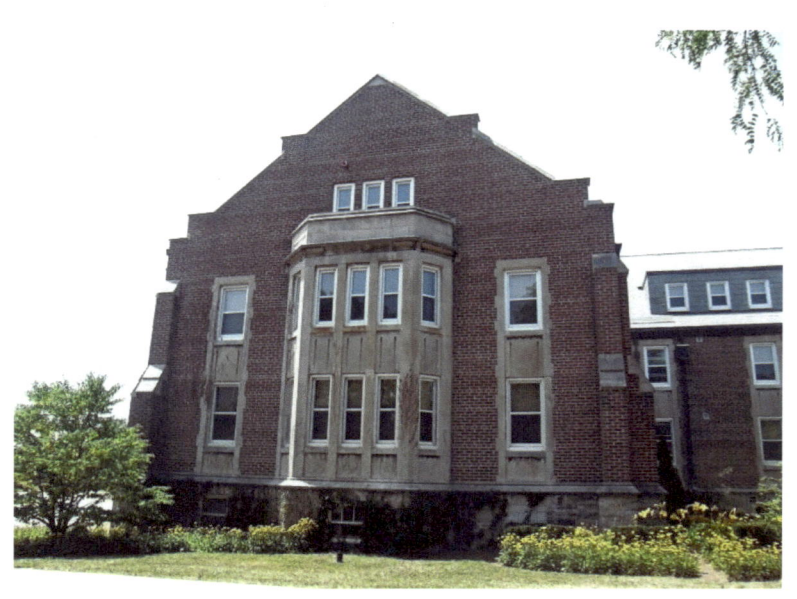

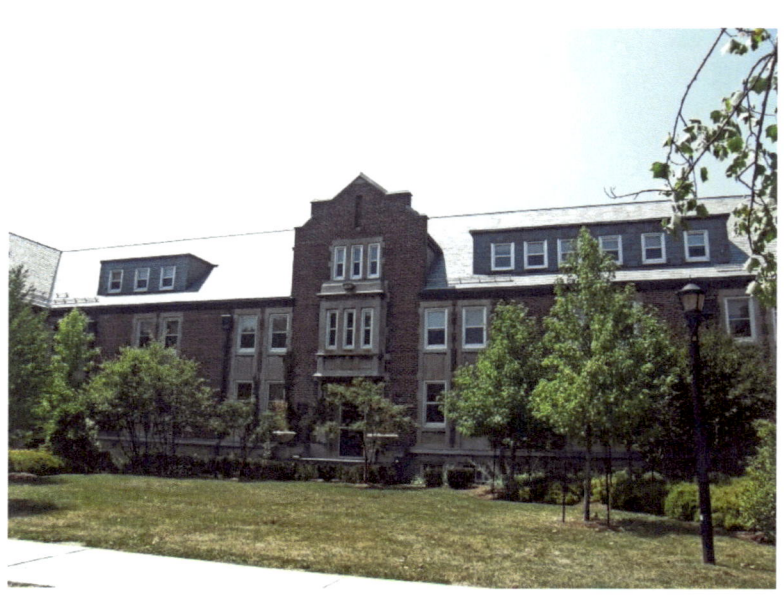

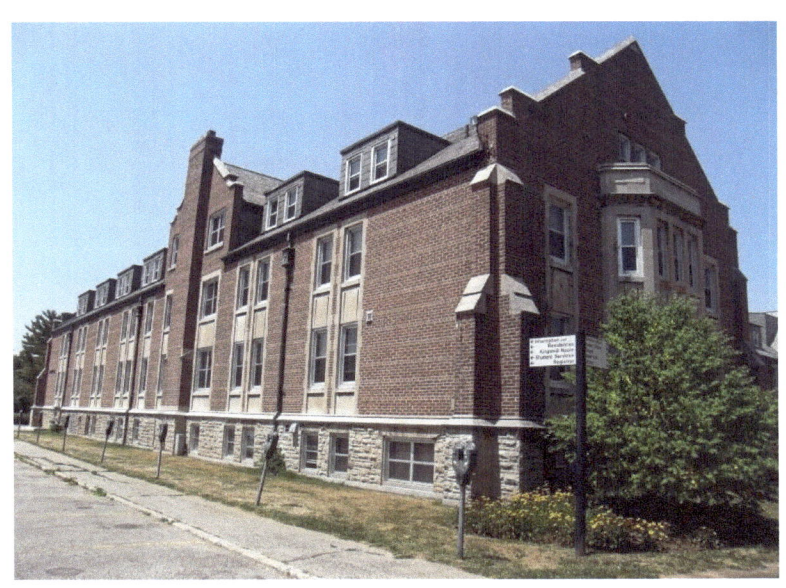

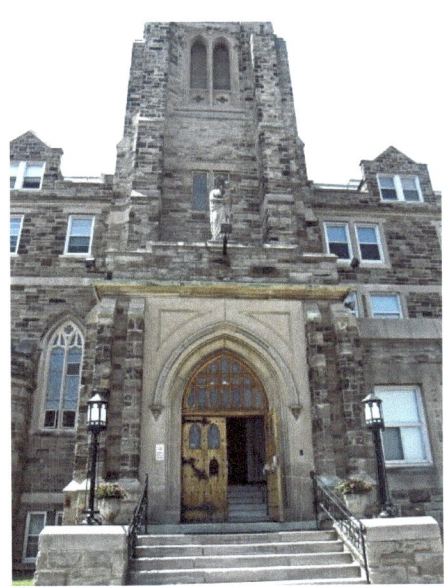

Brescia Residence – dichromatic brickwork

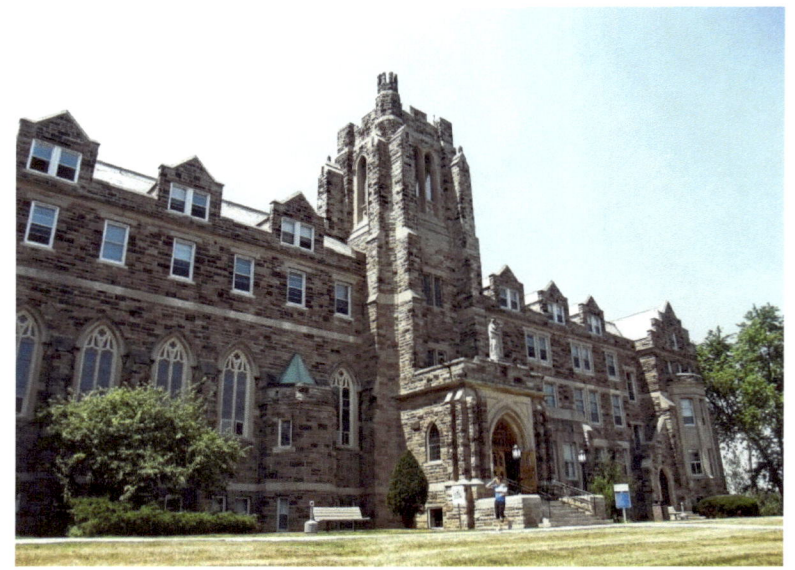

Brescia Residence – nuns lived in the left portion, students in the right; as the nuns died and no new ones took their places, the remainder of the building became residence for students

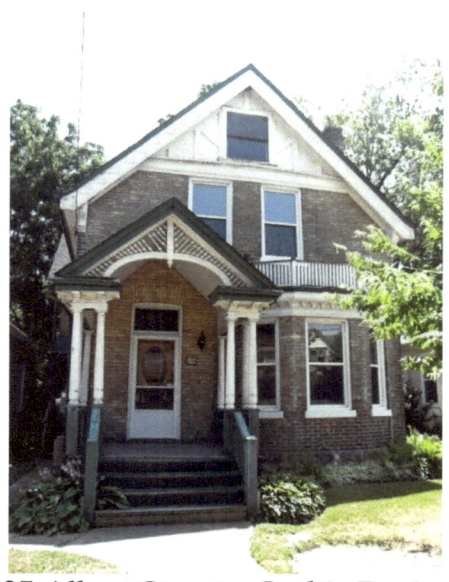

135 Albert Street – Gothic Revival

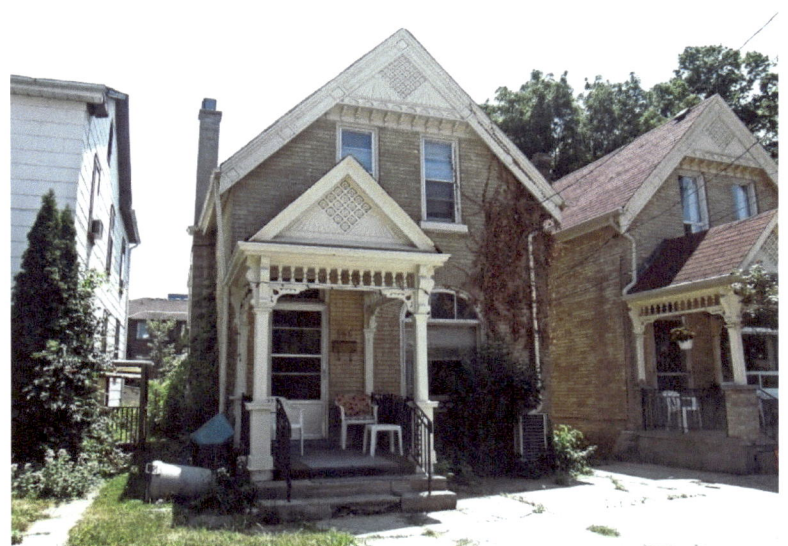

145 Albert Street – Gothic Revival

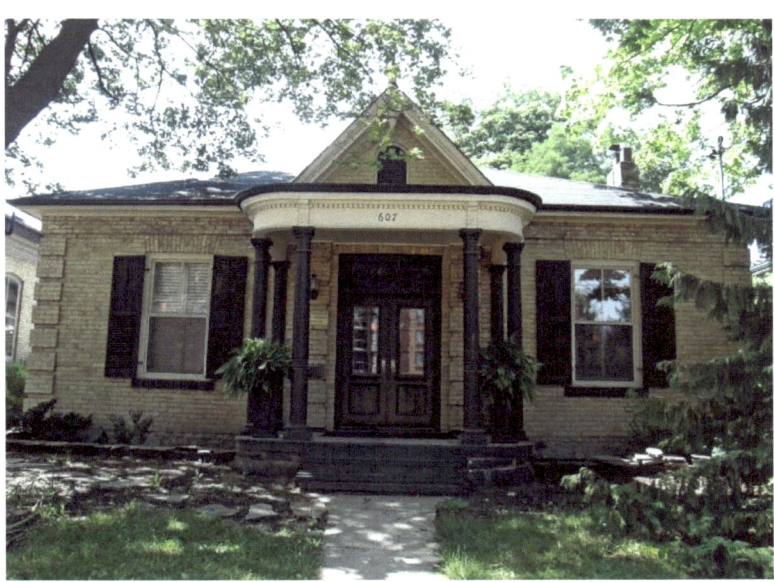

607 Ridout Street - Gothic Revival Cottage in yellow brick

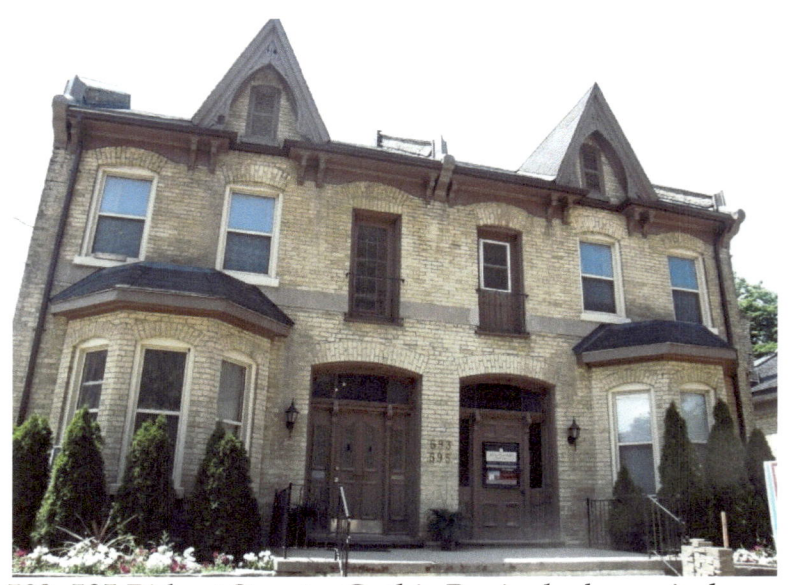

593, 595 Ridout Street – Gothic Revival – bay windows, cornice brackets

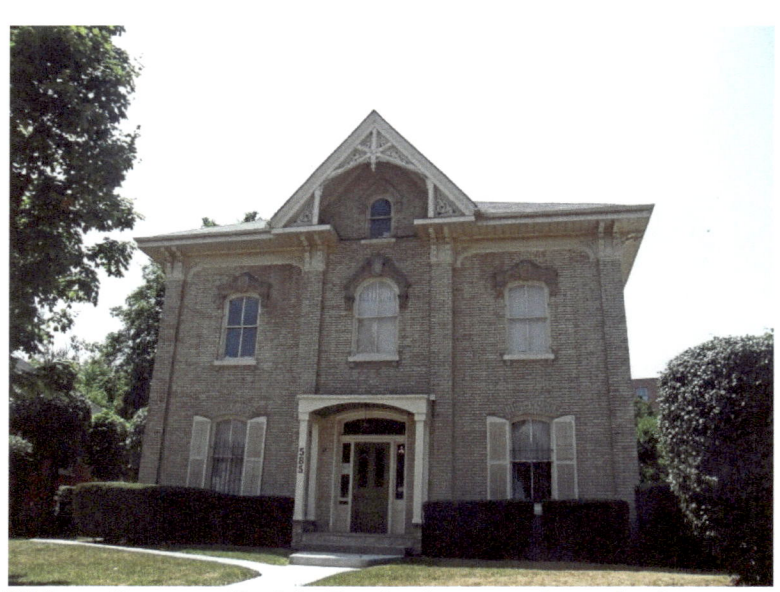

585 Ridout Street – Gothic Revival – vergeboard trim on gable, cornice brackets, decorative window hoods and keystones

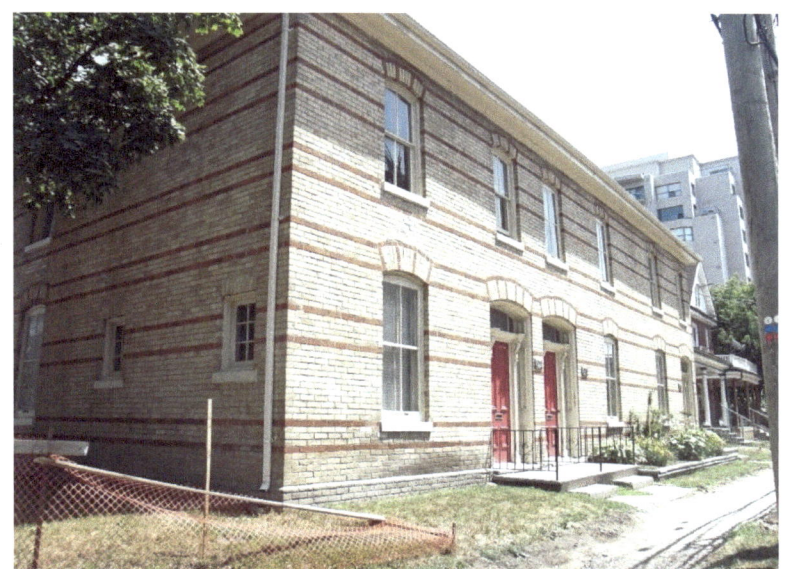

568-570 Ridout Street - dichromatic brickwork using two colours of brick.

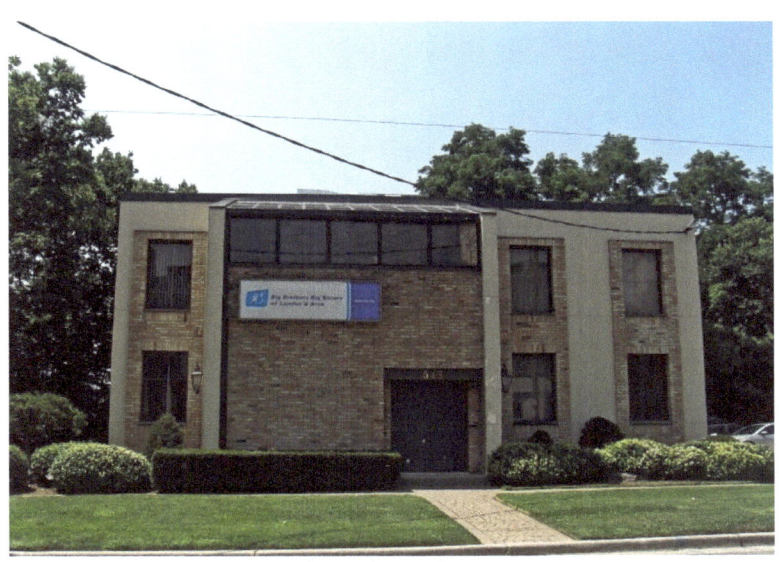

543 Ridout Street
Big Brothers Big Sisters of London & Area

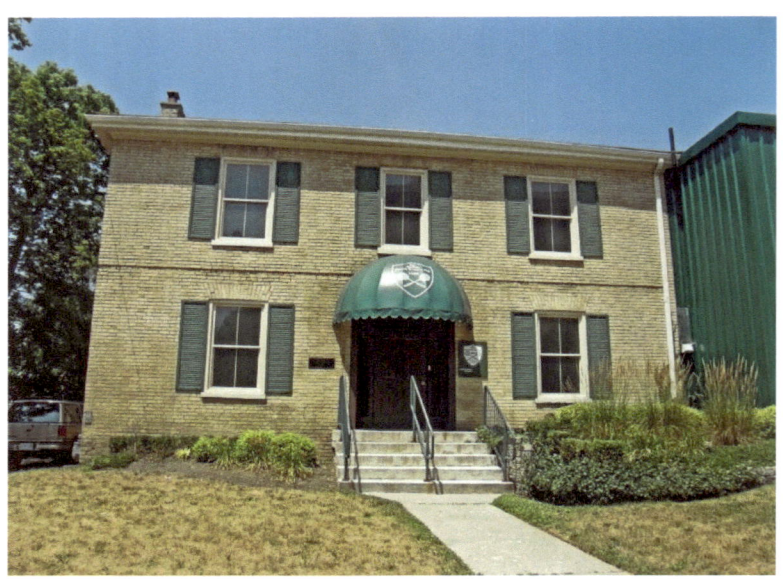

The London Squash Club – 1966
Italianate style

Josiah Blackburn, son of a Congregationalist minister, was born in London, England where he gained some experience in journalism. He immigrated to Canada West (now Ontario) in 1850 and joined the staff of The Star in Paris. Two years later he purchased a small London weekly, The Canadian Free Press, which became a weekly later called the London Free Press. He controlled the Ingersoll Chronicle and helped found The Mail in Toronto.

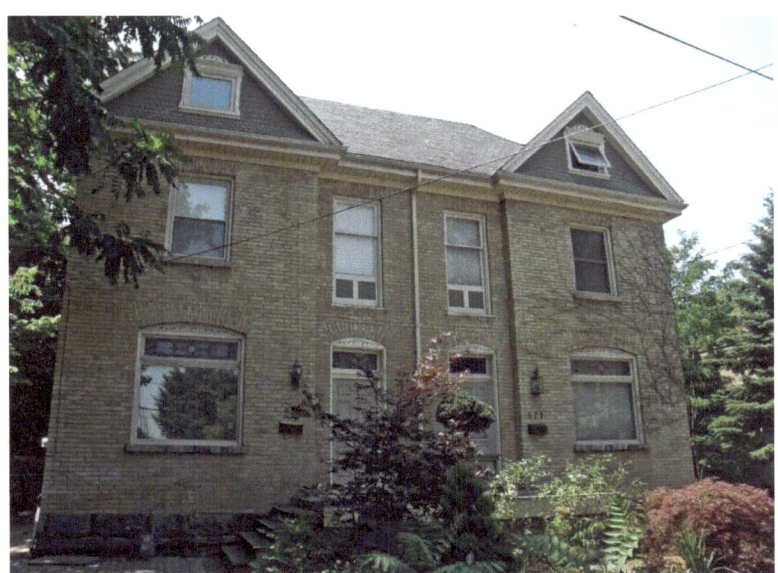

569-571 Ridout Street

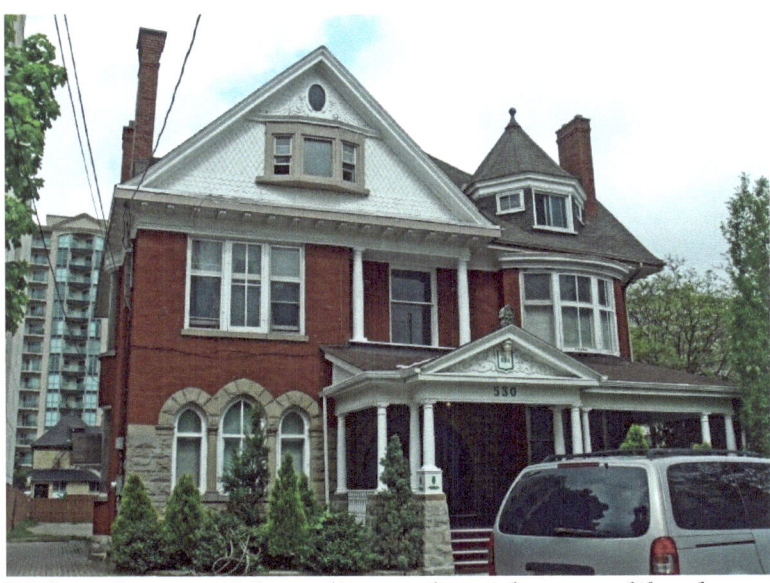

530 Ridout Street – Edwardian style with turret-like dormer in attic with cone-shaped roof

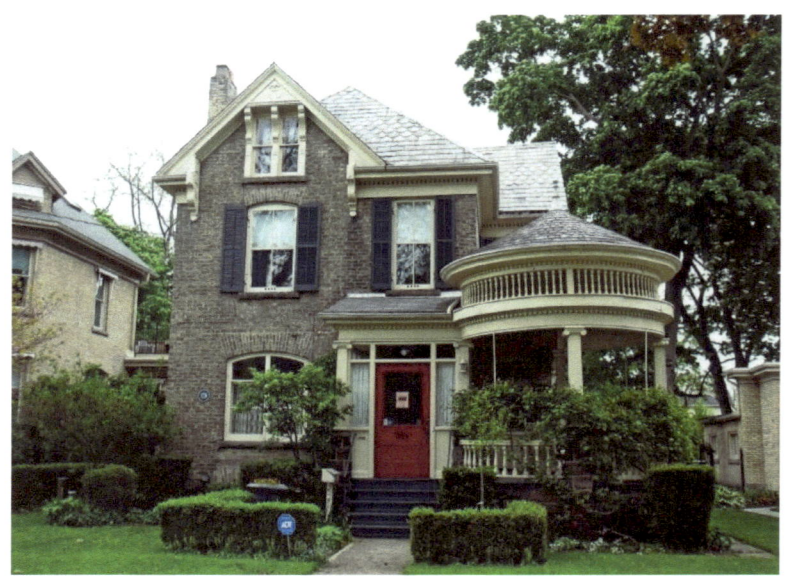

#784

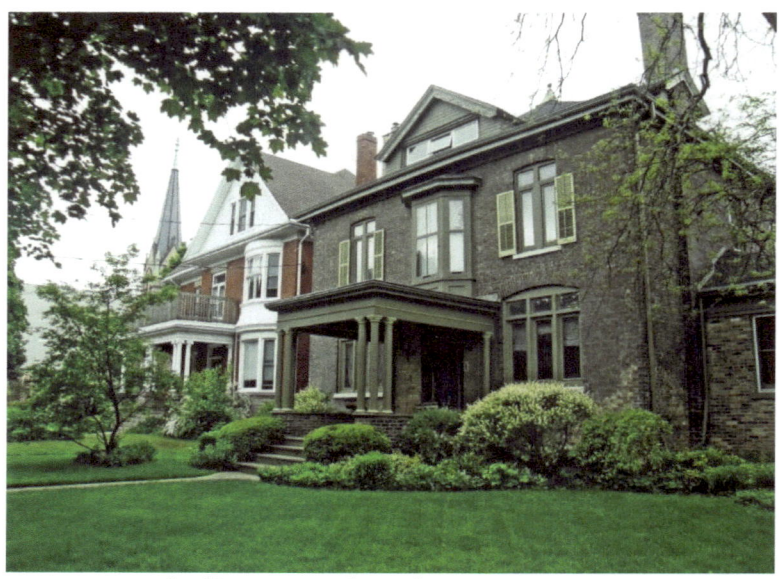

Italianate style – dormer in attic

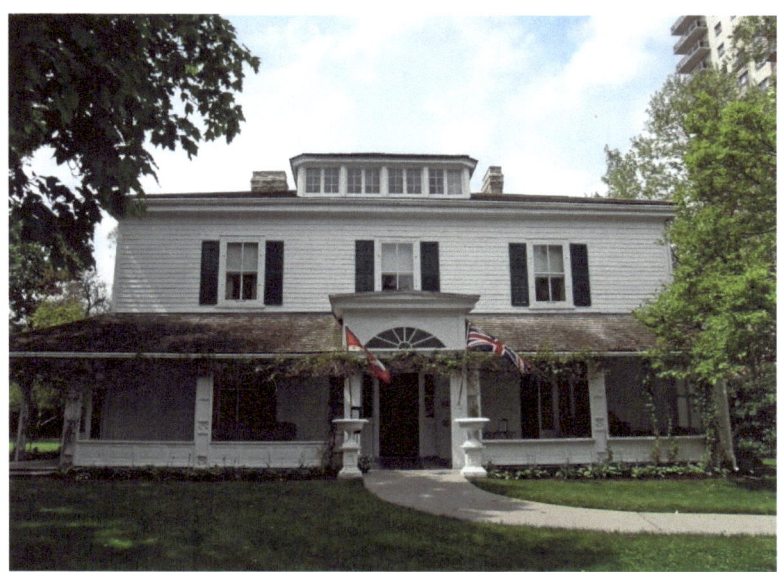

481 Ridout Street

Eldon House was built in 1834 by Captain John Harris, treasurer of the London district. This is London's oldest remaining house. With his wife Amelia, daughter of Samuel Ryerse, Harris came to London after the District Offices were moved here from Vittoria. For many years Eldon House was a centre of London's cultural and social life.

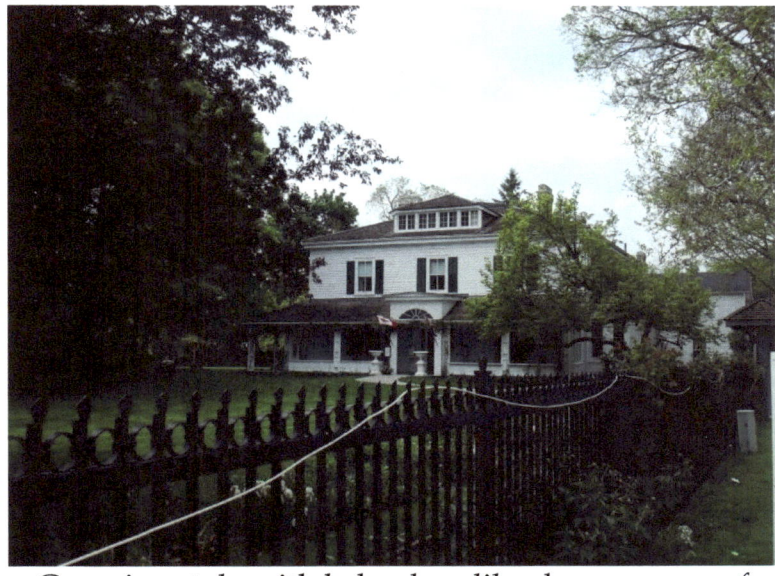

Georgian style with belvedere-like dormer on roof

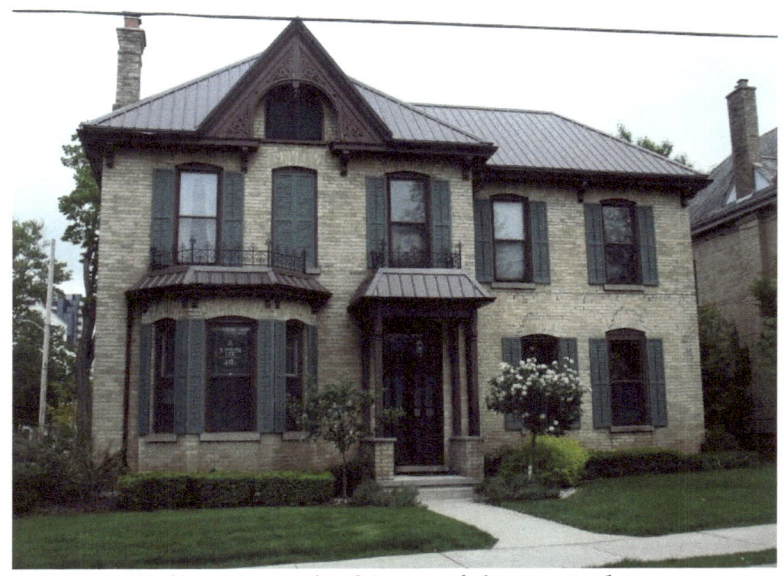

Italianate style, hip roof, bay window

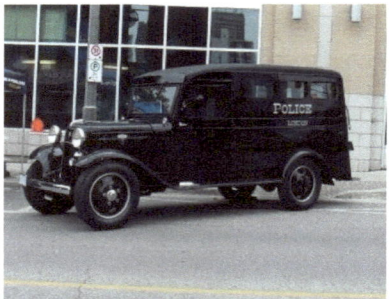

London Police Car

The Ridout Street Complex includes several of London's oldest buildings, with the earliest built in 1835. These buildings include residential, commercial and industrial premises intermingled on one of the city's main streets. The group of structures became known as "Bankers Row" with the presence of five branch offices here. John Labatt Limited restored three structures to preserve this rich heritage.

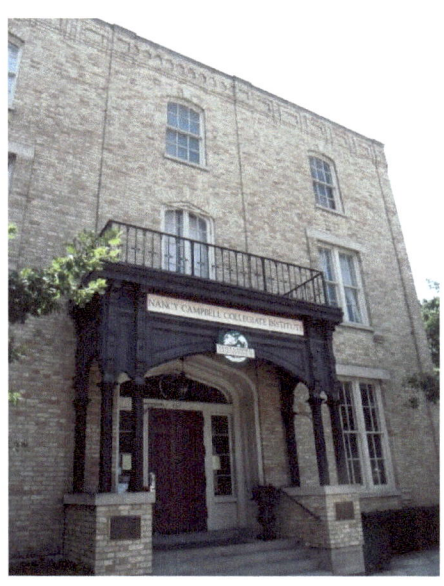

#451 - Nancy Campbell Collegiate Institute

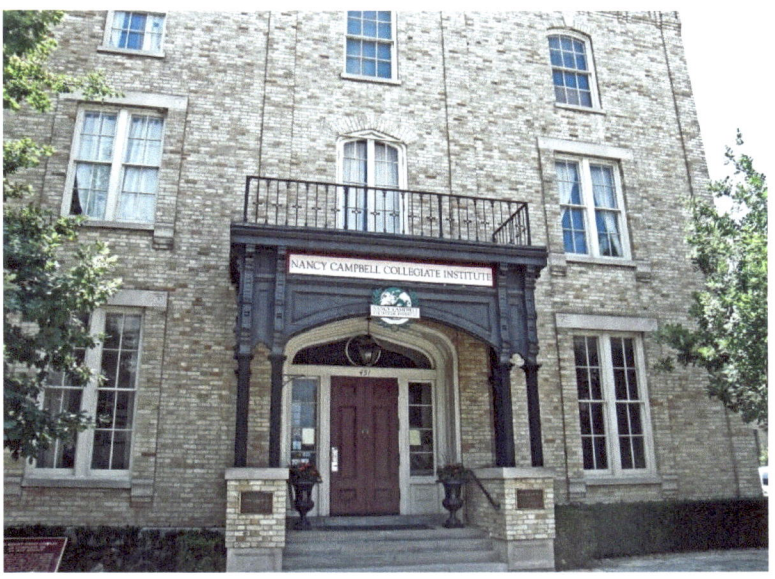

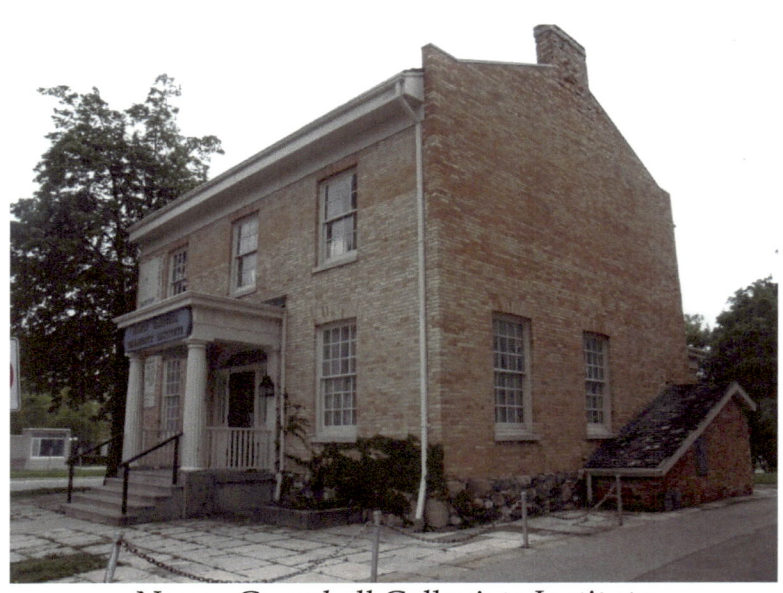

Nancy Campbell Collegiate Institute
Ridout Street

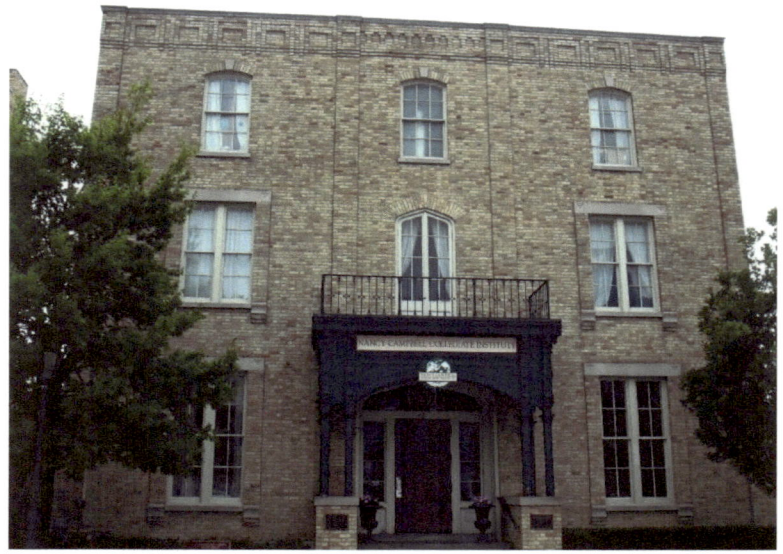

451 Ridout Street
Restored by John Labatt Limited in 1970
Formerly occupied by banks from 1838, private residences, and a private
school (1887-1919)

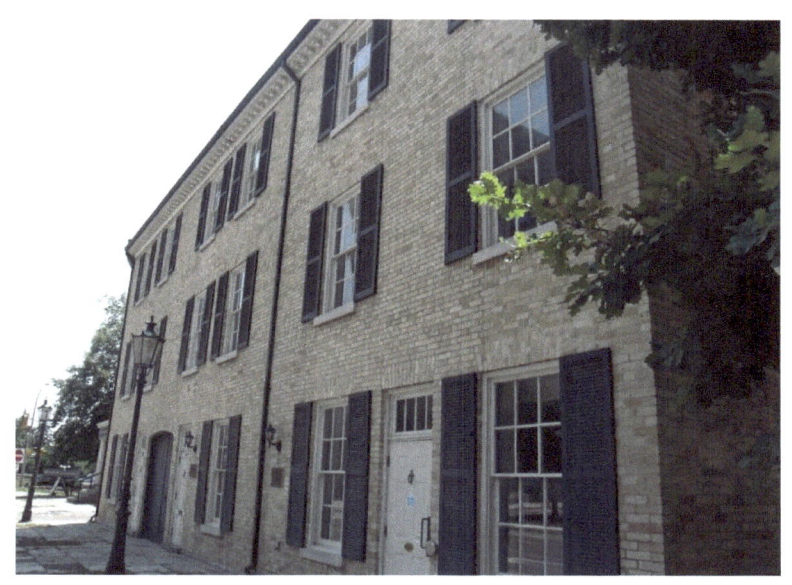

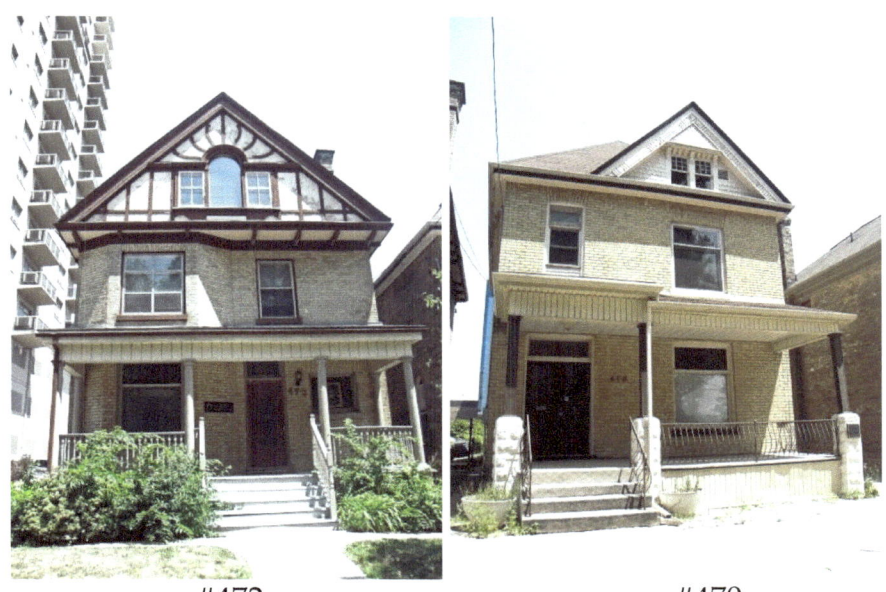

#472
Edwardian/Tudor style,
Palladian window

#470

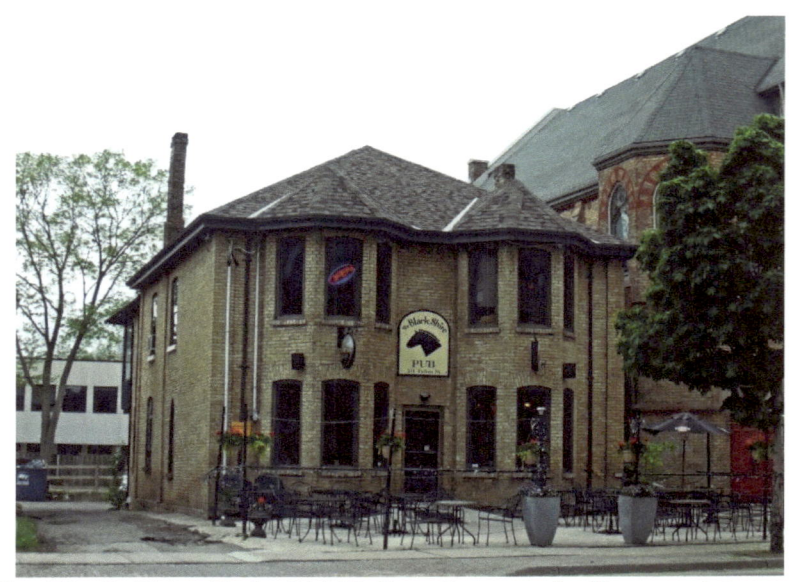

The Black Shire Pub, 511 Talbot Street – Italianate, hip roof

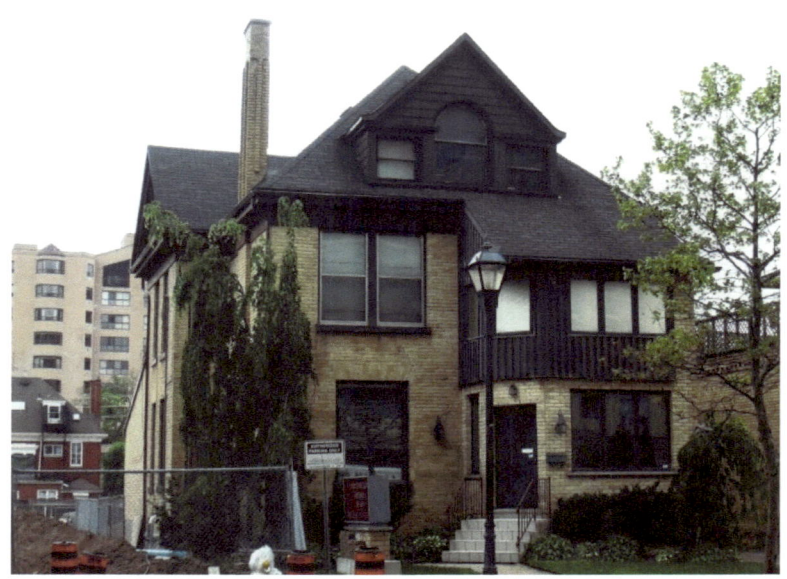

Italianate style, dormer in the attic

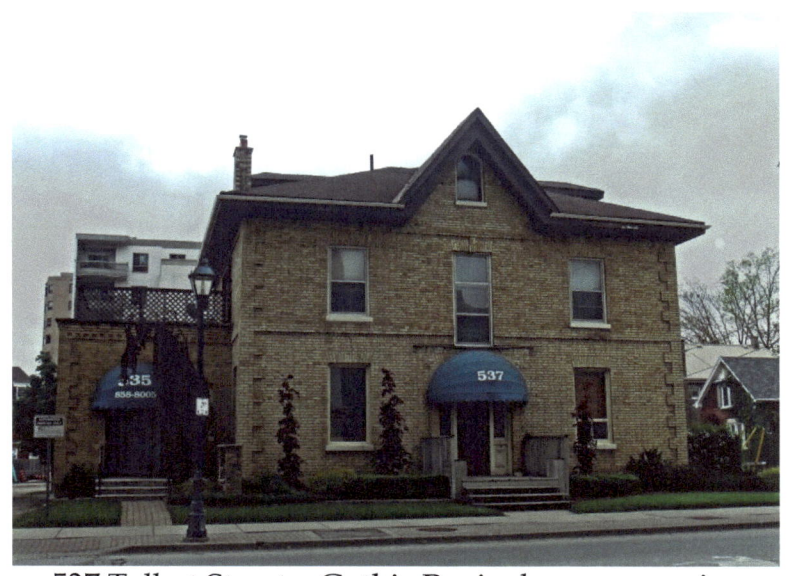

537 Talbot Street – Gothic Revival, corner quoins

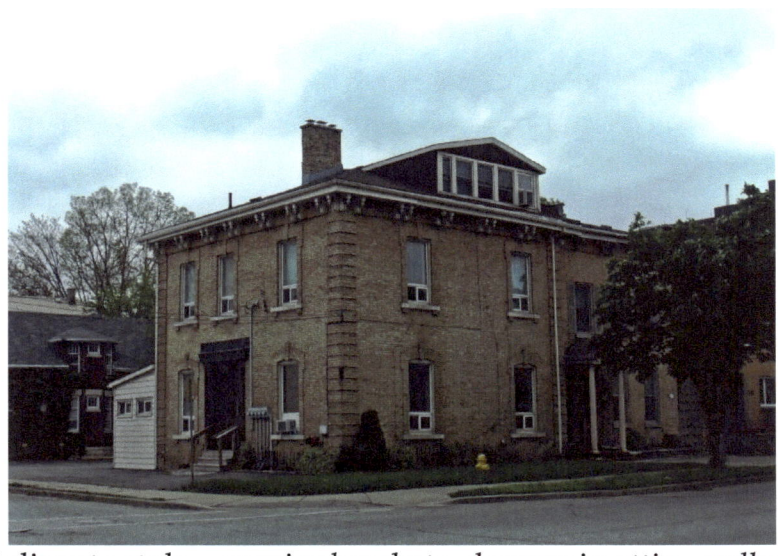

Italianate style – cornice brackets, dormer in attic – yellow
brick, corner quoins

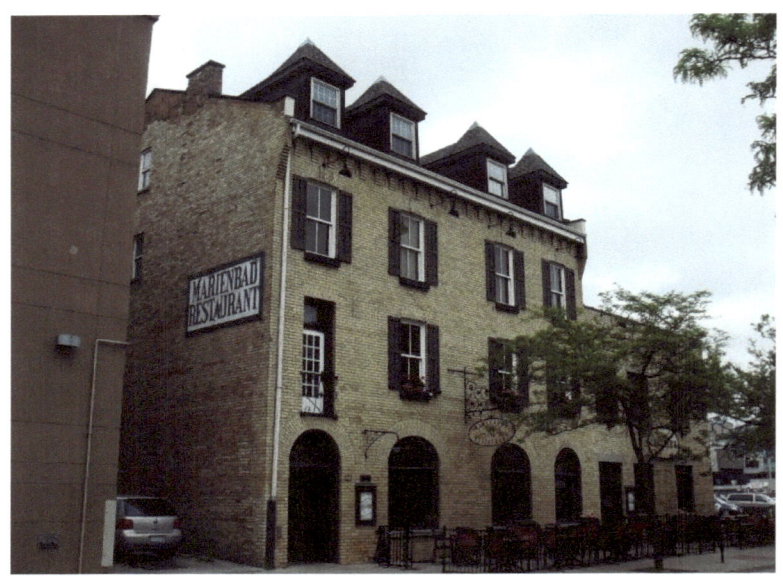

Marienbad Restaurant, 122 Carling Street – Italianate, dormers in attic

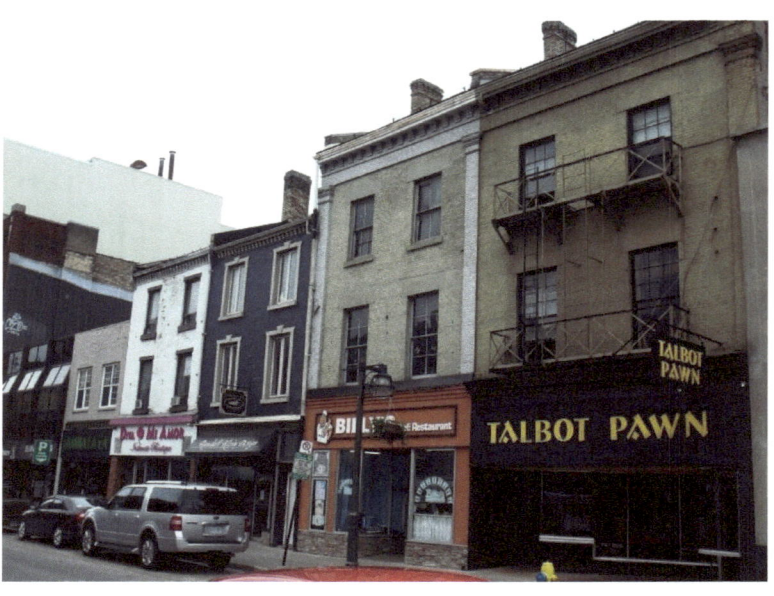

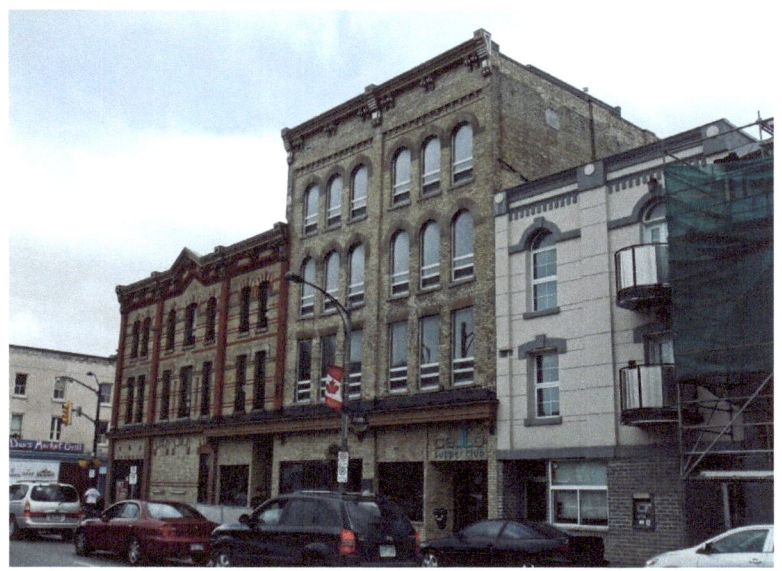

Downtown – dentil moulding, cornice brackets, window voussoirs and keystones

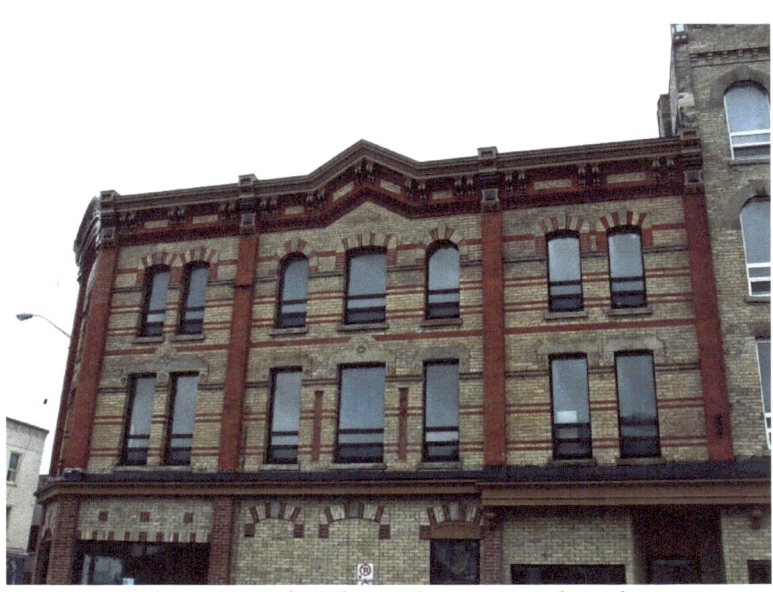

Dichromatic brickwork, cornice brackets

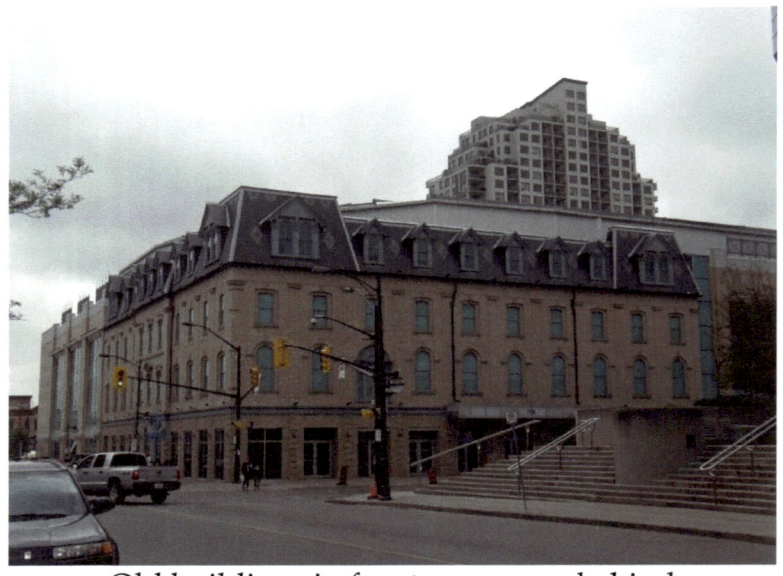

Old buildings in front, new ones behind
– corner of Dundas Street – mansard roof, dormers

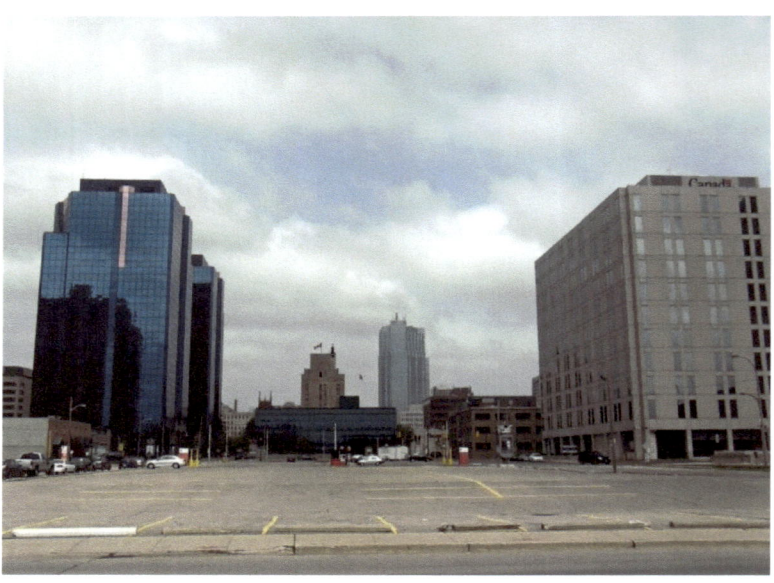

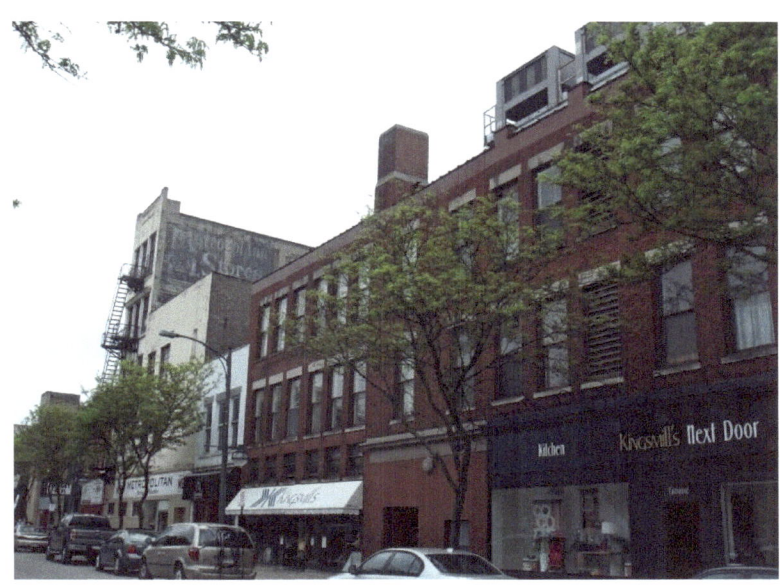

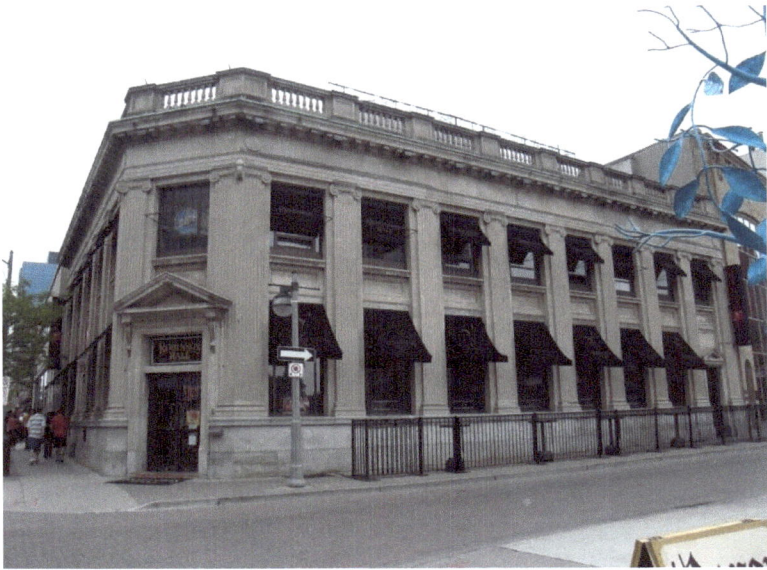

Robinson Hall – spindle railing around rooftop, capitals on the pillars

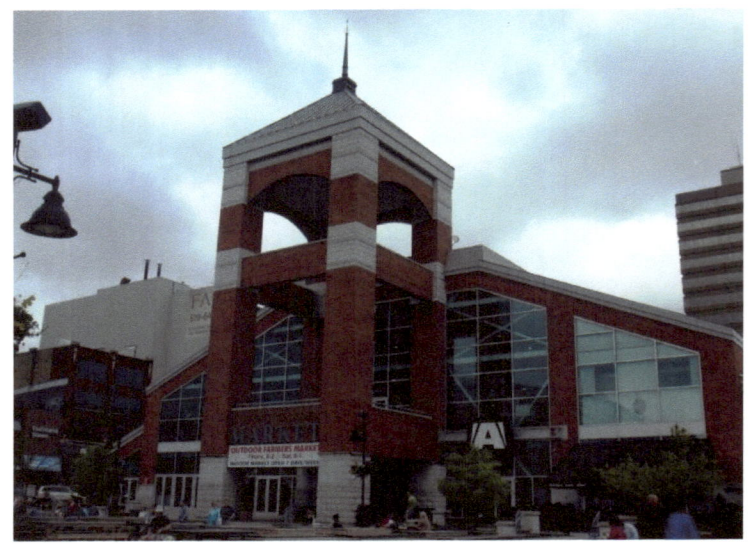

Covent Garden Market

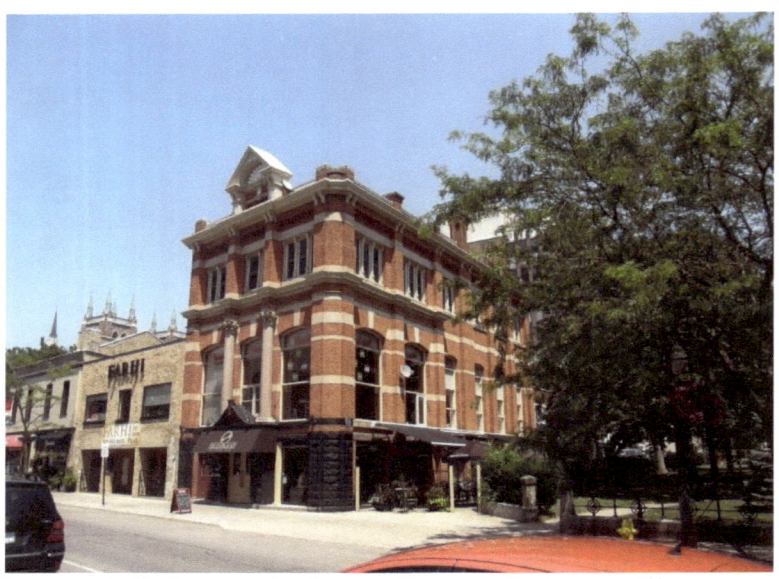

Dichromatic brickwork, decorative capitals on pillars, cornice brackets

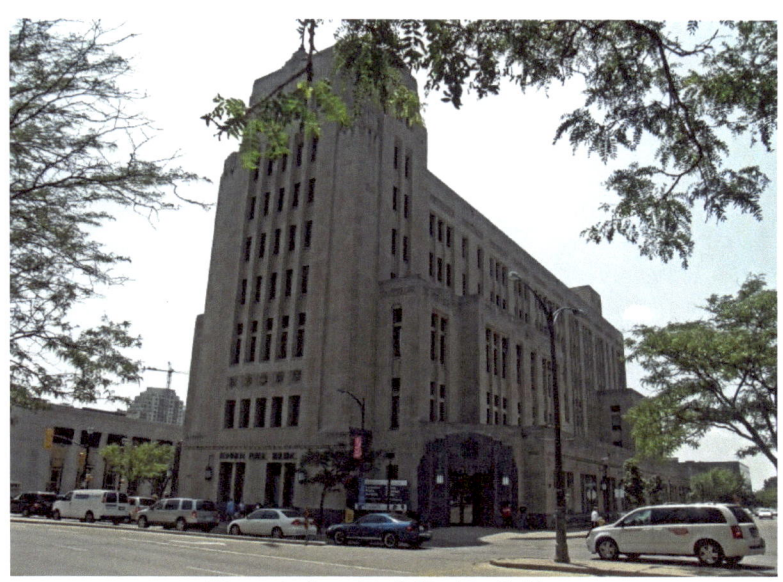

Dominion Public Building

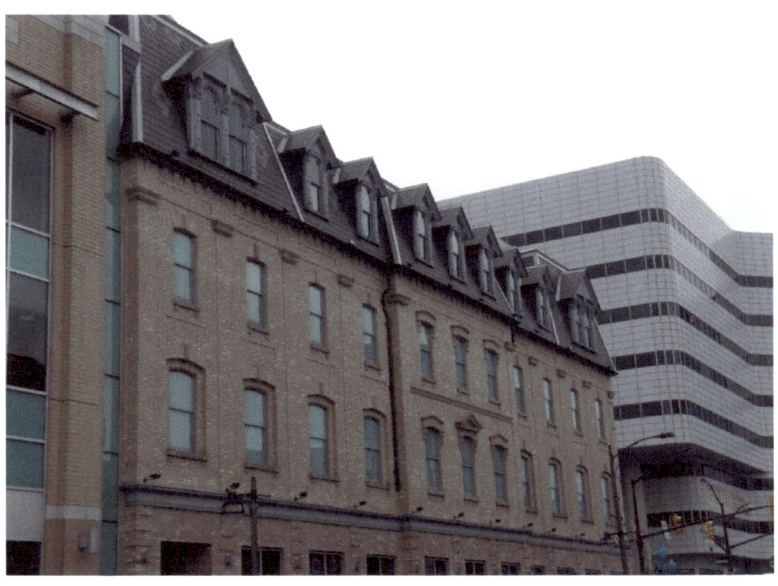

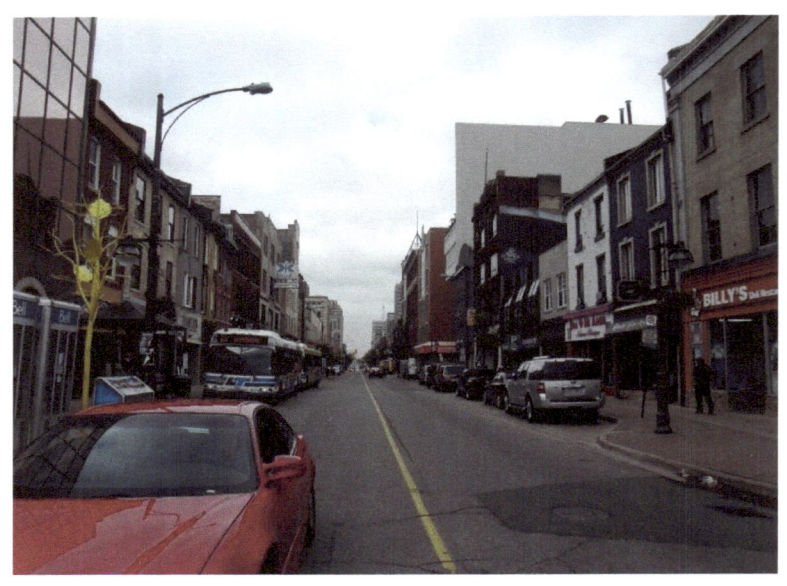

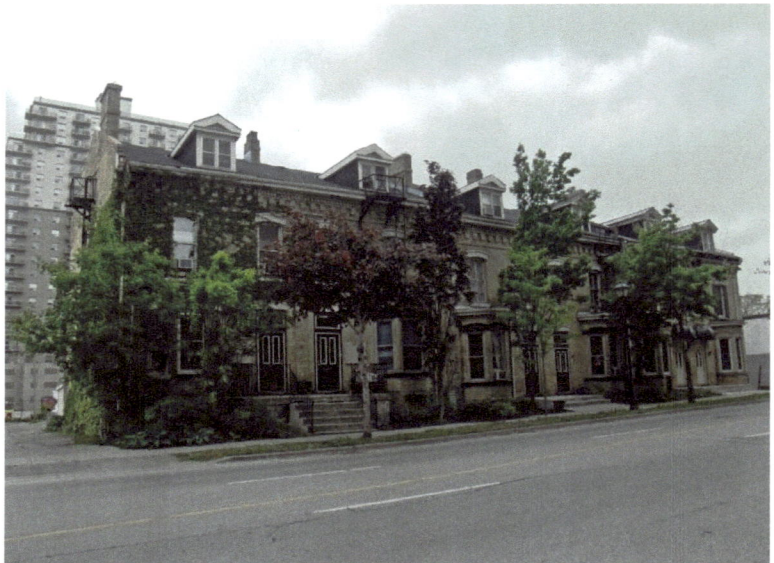

Dormers in attic, dentil moulding under cornice

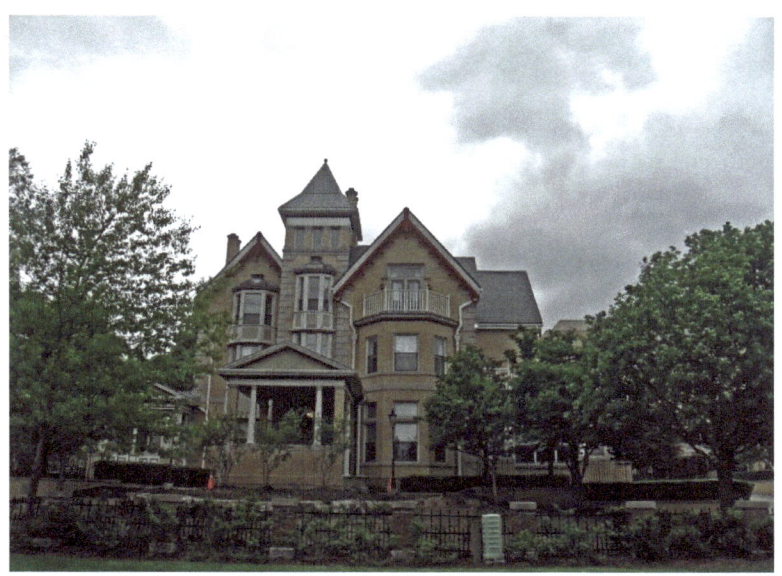

Queen Anne style – tower with cone-shaped cap, verge board trim

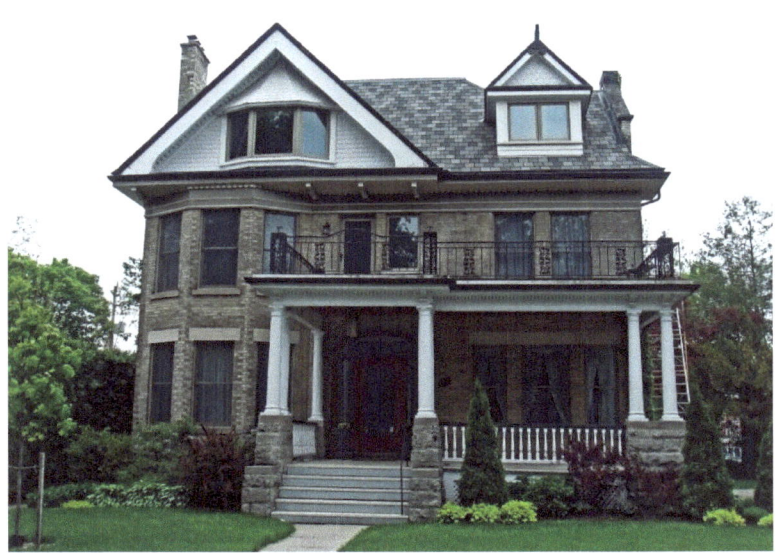

Italianate style with dormer in attic, two-and-a-half storey tower-like bay, balcony on second floor

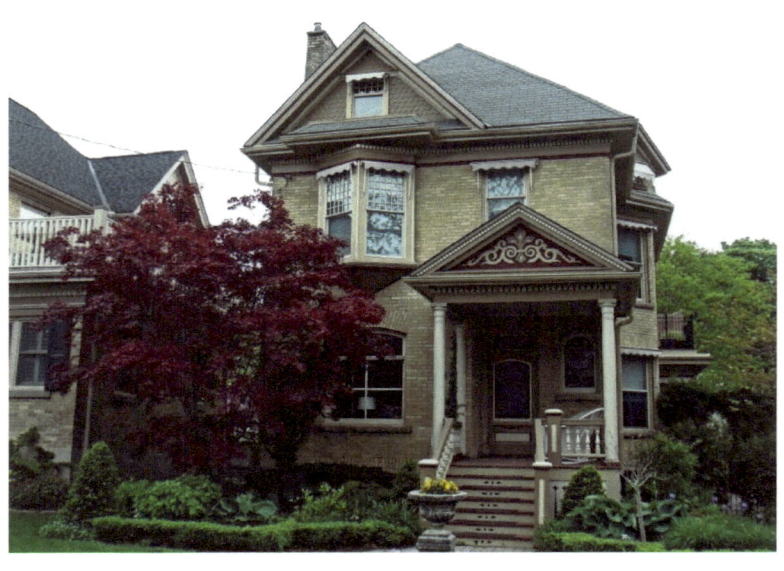

Italianate style – hip roof, pediment with decorated tympanum, dormers in attic

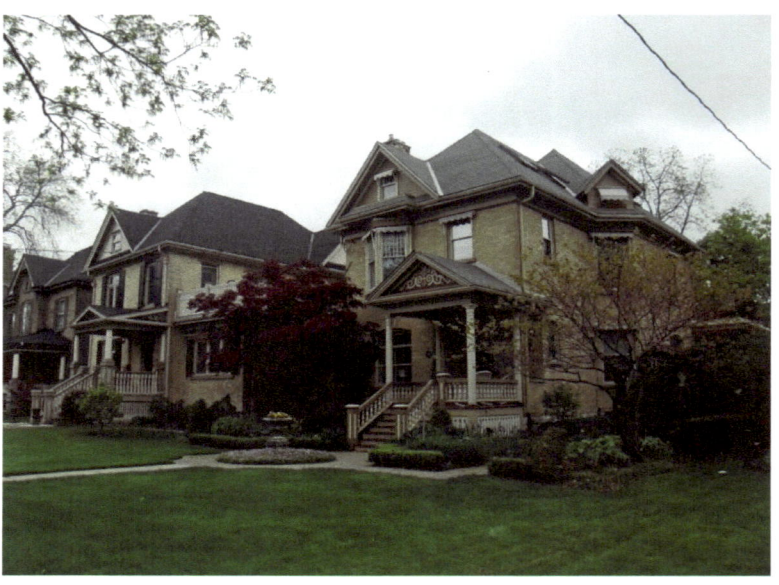

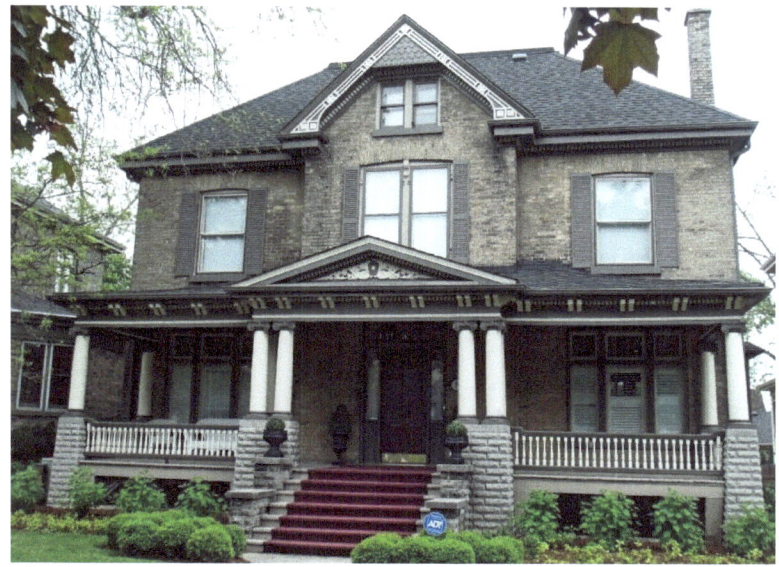

Italianate style with two-and-a-half storey tower-like bay,
pediment above verandah

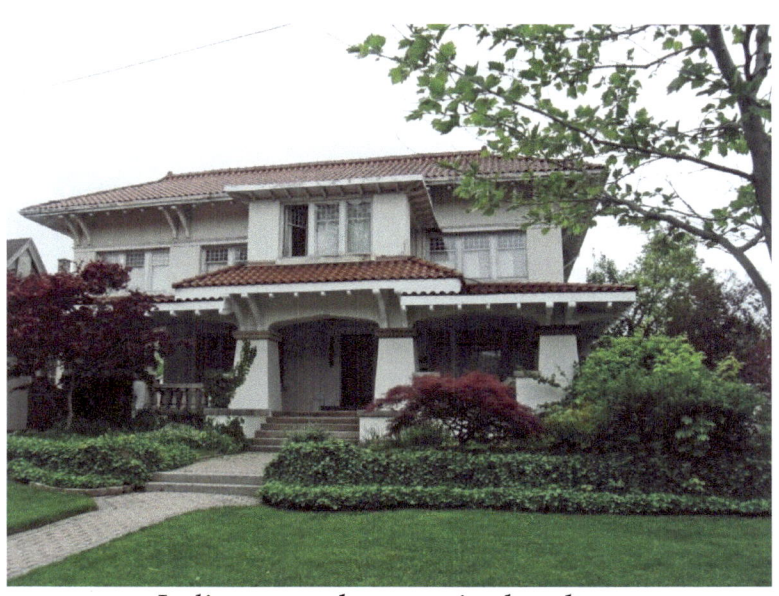

Italianate style – cornice brackets

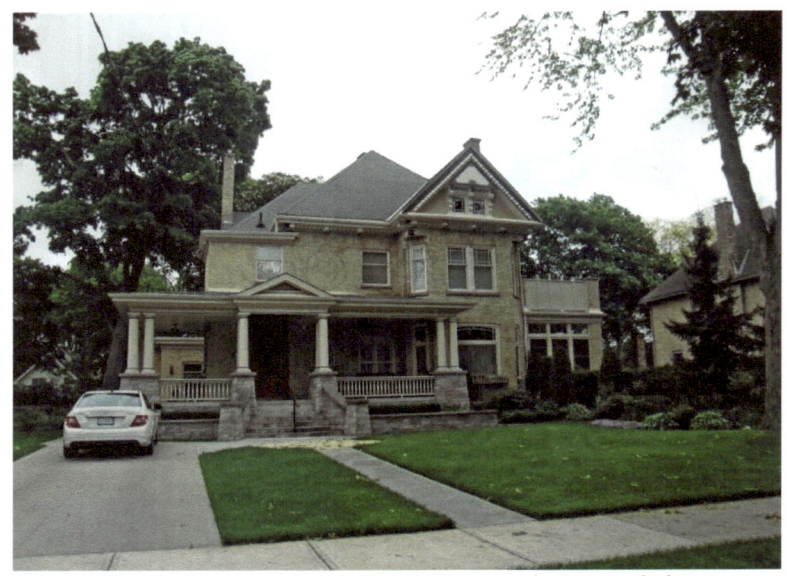

Italianate style – wrap-around verandah

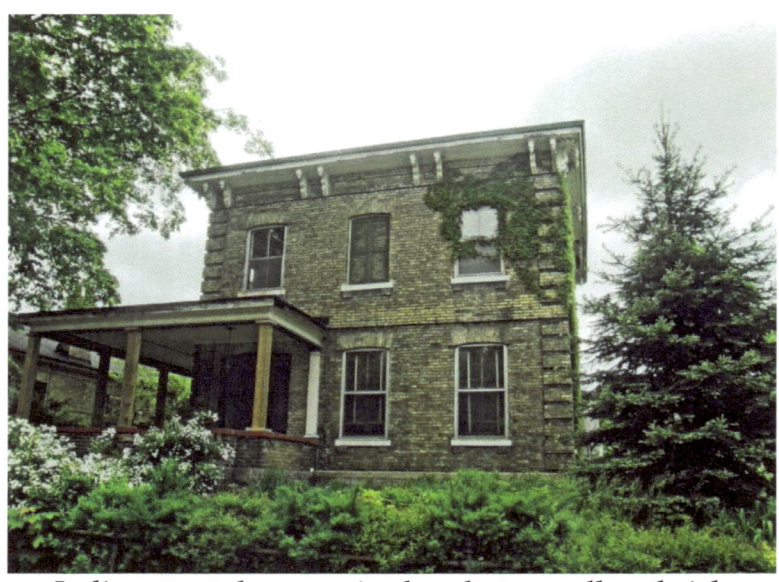

Italianate style – cornice brackets – yellow brick

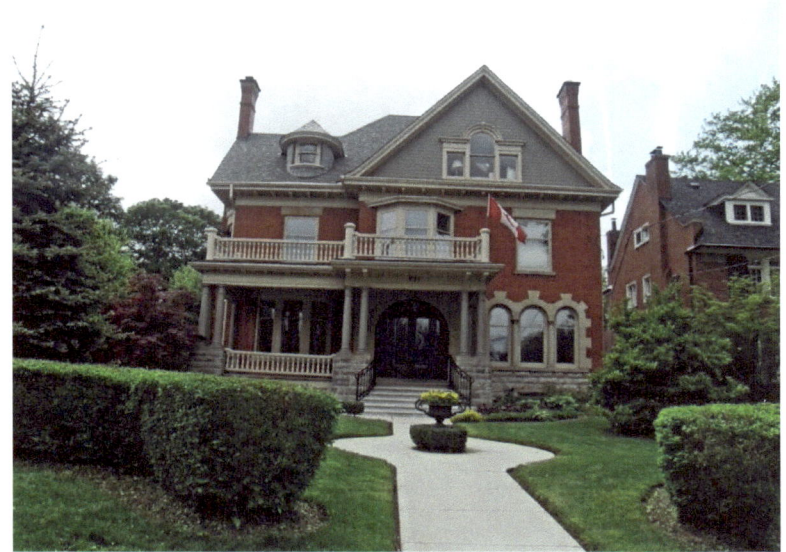

\# 651 – Edwardian style, palladian window, turret-shaped dormer in attic

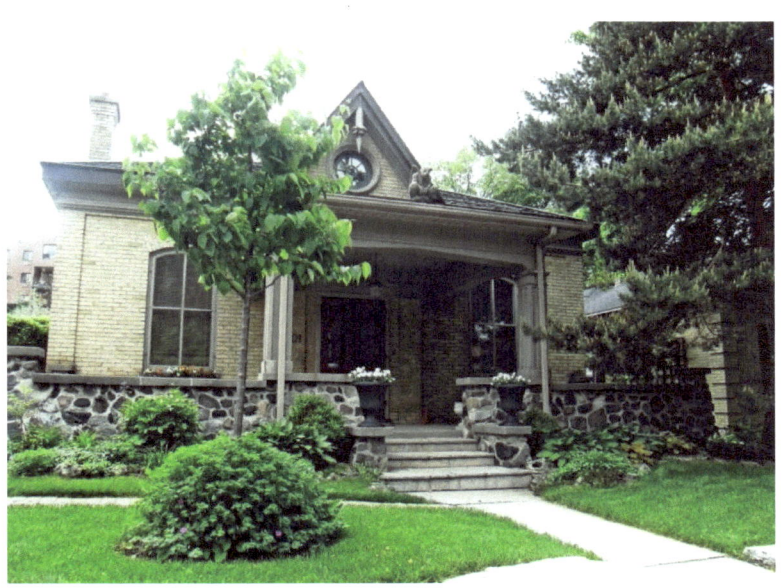

Gothic Revival

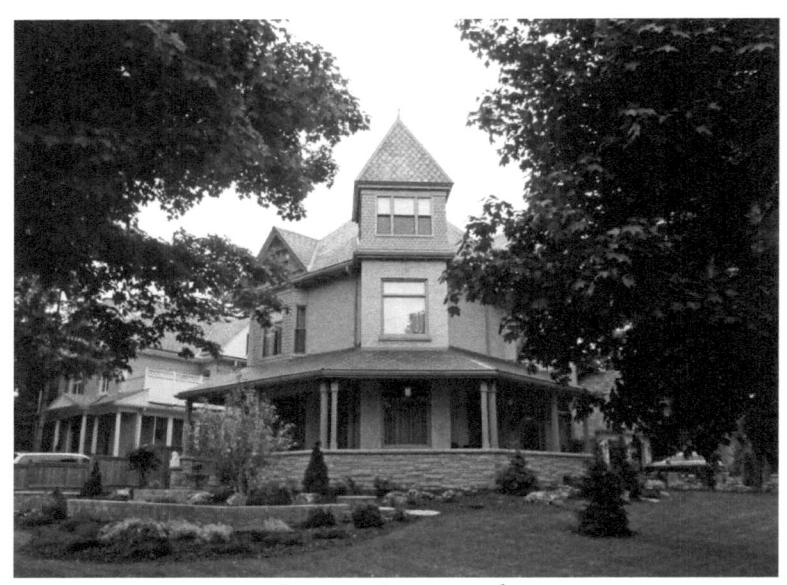

Queen Anne style

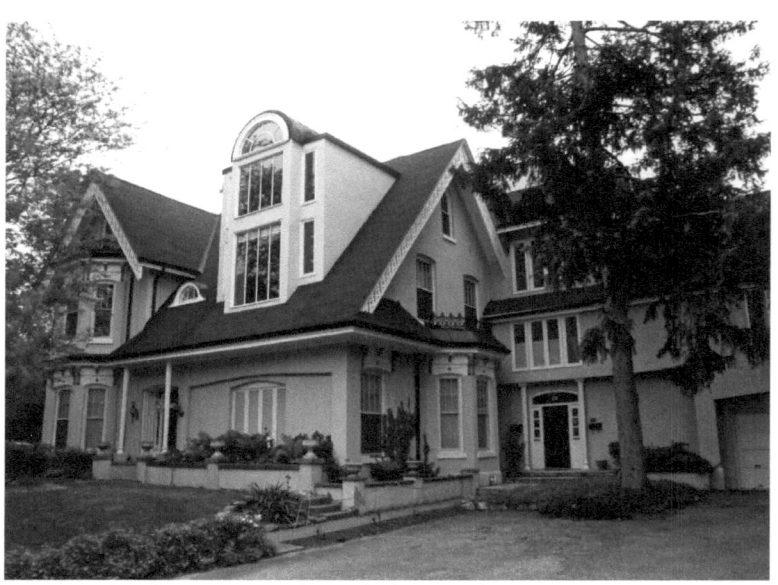

Gothic Revival with large dormer in attic

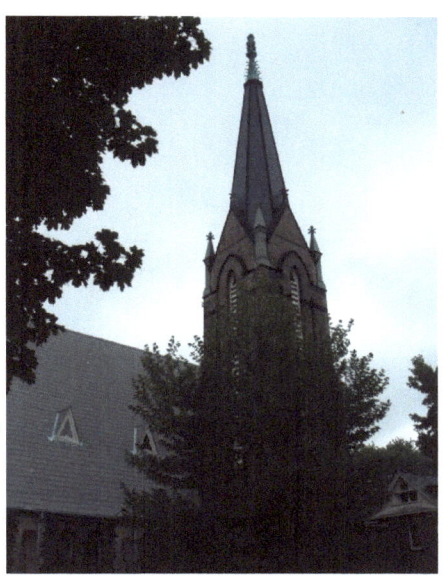

The Anglican Church of St. John the Evangelist
Corner of St. James and Wellington Streets
Established 1888 – Gothic Revival

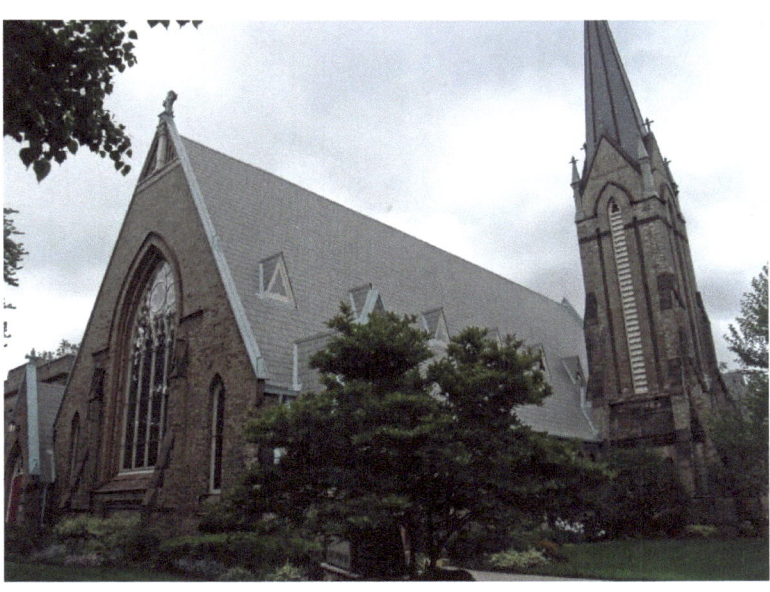

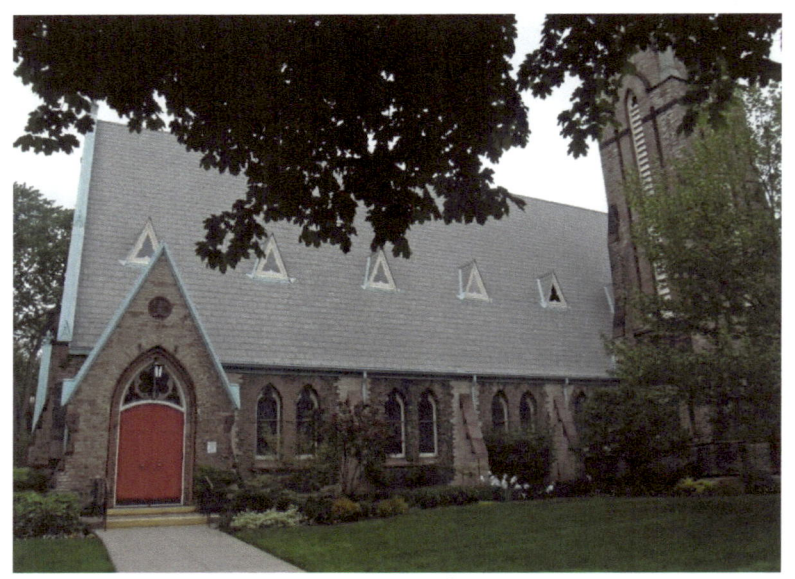

Lancet windows

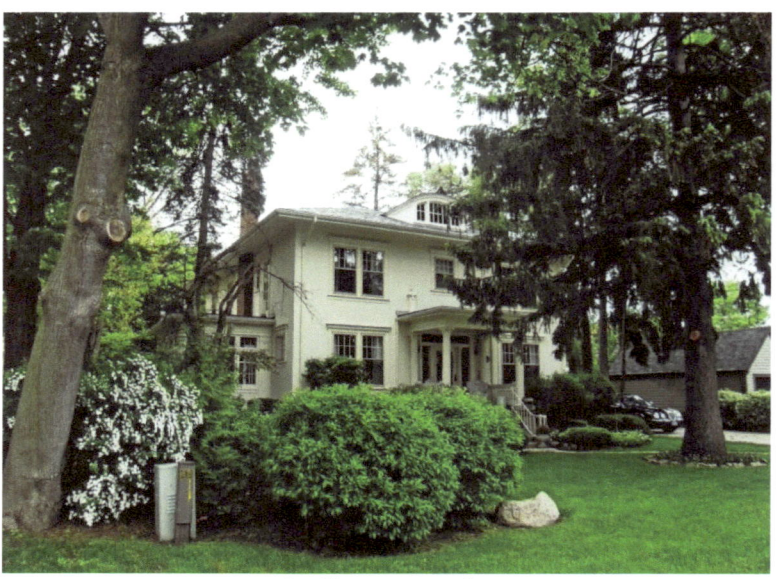

Italianate style

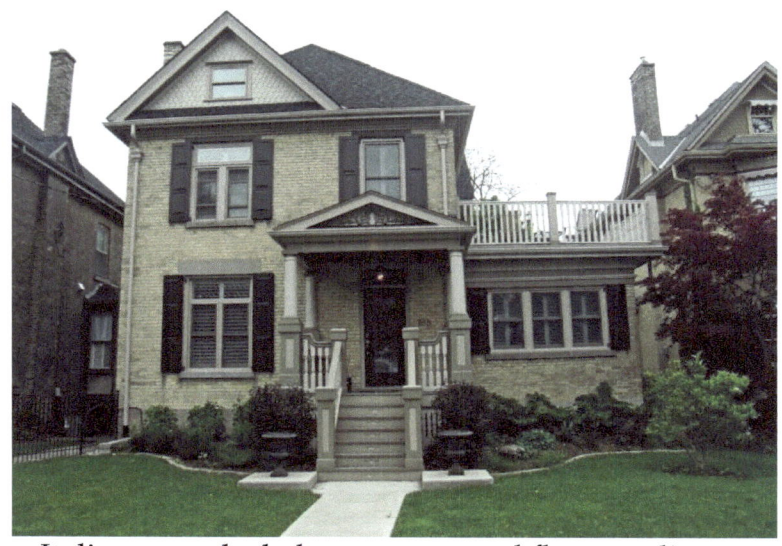

Italianate style, balcony on second floor, pediment

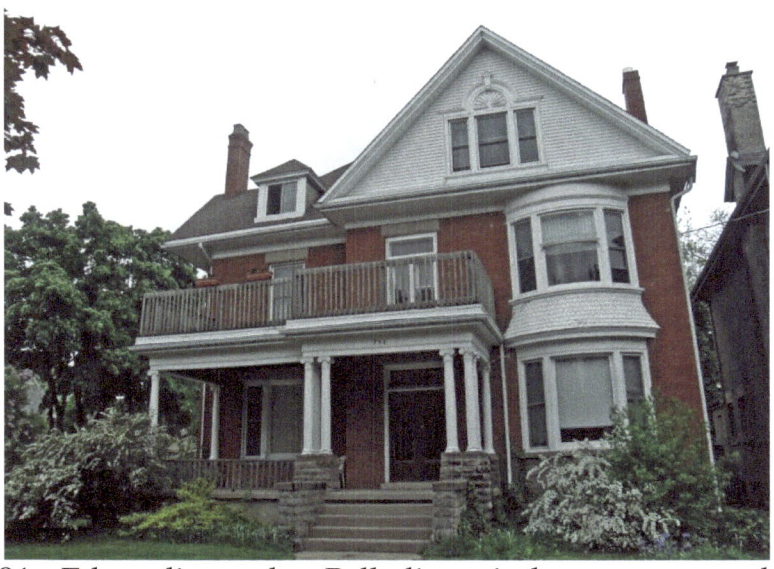

#794 – Edwardian style – Palladian window, two-storey bay windows

Architectural Terms

Brackets: a decorative or weight-bearing structural element which forms a right angle with one side against a wall and the other under a projecting surface such as an eave or roof. Example: 593, 595 Ridout Street, Page 50	
Buttress: a masonry structure built against or projecting from a wall which serves to support or reinforce the wall. In Canadian architecture, they are sometimes used for decoration. Example: Elmwood Avenue Presbyterian Church, Page 10	
Cornice: originally the wooden overhang of the roof. With the use of stone, brick, iron and steel, the cornice is any projecting shelf at the top of a ceiling or roof. They can be very decorative. Example: 585 Ridout Street, Page 50	
Cornice Return: decorative element on the end of a gable. Example: 62 Elmwood Avenue, Page 14	
Capital: The uppermost finish or decoration on a column. Example: Page 66	
Dentil Moulding: an even series of rectangles used as ornamental decoration in cornices. Example: Page 63	

Dichromatic brickwork: the use of two colours of brick, tile or slate to decorate a façade. Example: Downtown, Page 63	
Dormer: (French for "sleep") a gable end window that pierces through the plane of a sloping roof surface to create usable space in the top floor or attic of a building by adding headroom. Example: Marienbad Restaurant, 122 Carling Street, Page 62	
Finial: ornament added to the top of a gable, pinnacle, canopy or spire – a Gothic element. Example: Central Avenue, Page 34	
Gable: the triangular portion of a wall between the edges of a sloping roof. Example: 96 Askin Street, Page 24	
Hipped Roof: a roof where all sides slope downwards to the walls with no gables. Example: The Black Shire Pub, 511 Talbot Street, Page 60	

Keystones and Voussoirs: a voussoir is a wedge-shaped element used in building an arch. A keystone is the central stone that locks all the stones into position, allowing the arch to bear weight. A keystone is often enlarged and embellished. Example: 585 Ridout Street, Page 50	
Lancet Window: a tall, narrow window with a pointed arch at its top. Example: Saint James Wesminster Anglican Church, 115 Askin Street, Page 21	
Mansard Roof: This style was popularized by Francois Mansart (1598-1666), an accomplished architect of the French Baroque period and especially fashionable during the Second French Empire (1852-1870). This roof is almost flat on the top section, with two slopes on each of its sides with the lower slope at a steeper angle than the upper and having dormer windows. Example: corner of Dundas Street, Page 64	
Palladian Window: a large window that is divided into three sections with the centre section larger than the two side sections and usually arched. Example: Page 77	

Pediment: a triangular section above the horizontal structure (entablature), typically supported by columns. The inside of the triangle is called the tympanum. Example: 56 Elmwood Avenue, Page 16	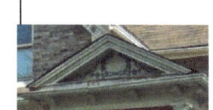
Quoin: masonry blocks at the corner of a wall, often a decorative feature, usually larger or of a different colour than the rest of the wall. Example: Talbot Street, Page 61	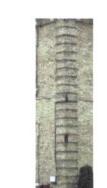
Tower: A circular, square, or octagonal vertical structure higher than the surrounding structure that is usually part of an existing building and is created either for extra defense or for a specific purpose such as a clock or a bell tower. Example: 70 Elmwood Avenue, Page 14	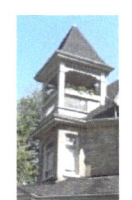
Rose Window: a circular window with ornamental tracery radiating from the centre. Example: St. Peter's Cathedral Basilica, 533 Clarence Street, Page 28	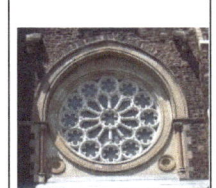
Verge boards: also called bargeboards – hang from the projecting end of a roof and are often elaborately carved and ornamented. Example: Elmwood Avenue, Page 15	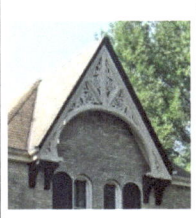

London's Building Styles

Georgian, before 1860 – This style began with the British King Georges in the 18th century. These buildings have balanced facades around a central door, medium-pitched gable roofs, and small paned windows. Example: 562 Waterloo Avenue, Page 40	
Regency Cottage, 1830-1860 – This style originated in England in 1815 and spread to Ontario later in the 19th century as British officers retired to Canada. It is a modest one-storey house with a low-pitched hip roof and has a symmetrical front façade. Example: 29 Elmwood Avenue, Page 20	
Gothic Revival, 1830-1890 – These decorative buildings have sharply-pitched gables with highly detailed verge boards, pointed-arch window openings, and dichromatic brickwork. It is a common style in Ontario. Example: Elmwood Avenue, Page 15	

Italianate, 1850-1900 – It has wide-bracketed eaves, belvederes, wrap-around verandahs. Example: Page 56	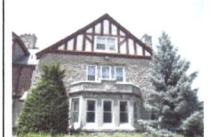
Tudor Revival – exposed timbers with stucco infill, multi-paned windows. Example: Huron College, Page 45	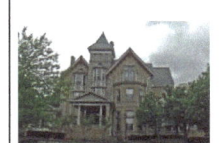
Queen Anne, 1885-1900 – This style is distinguished by an irregular outline featuring a combination of an offset tower, broad gables, projecting two-storey bays, verandahs, multi-sloped roofs, and tall, decorative chimneys. A mixture of brick and wood is common. Windows often have one large single-paned bottom sash and small panes in the upper sash. Example: Page 69	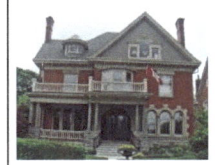
Edwardian, 1900-1930 – This style bridges the ornate and elaborate styles of the Victorian era and the simplified styles of the 20th century. Balanced facades, simple roof lines, dormer windows, large front porches, and smooth brick surfaces are its characteristics. Example: #651, Page 73